The Second
Answer Book

The Second
Answer Book

by

Samuel C. Gipp, Th.D., Ph.D.

DayStar Publishing
PO Box 464 • Miamitown, Ohio 45041

ISBN
9781942050186

Library of Congress Number
2020932966

Ministry site: samgipp.com
DayStar Publishing: daystarpublishing.com
You Tube Videos: Search - "sam gipp channel"
King James Videos - bigdealkjv.com

Printed by
Bible and Literature Missionary Foundation
2101 Highway 231 South • Shelbyville,TN 37160
website: biblelit.com

Books by this Author

The Answer Book

Gipp's Understandable History of the Bible

A Practical and Theological Study of The Book of Acts

A Practical and Theological Study of The Gospel of John

Living With Pain

Answers To the Ravings of a Mad Plunger

Reading and Understanding the Variations
Between the Critical Apparatuses of
Nestle's 25th and 26th Editions of
the *Novum Testamentum-Graece*

How To Minister To Youth

Selected Sermons (Vol. I - X)

Your Purpose for Existing

How To Get your Book Published

Fight On!

More Fight On! Stories

(Christian School materials)

Dedication

This Book is dedicated to:

People who are tired of having their faith in God's perfect Bible attacked, especially by those who claim to believe that very thing.

Young college students who innocently attend a "King James Bible-believing Bible college" who then have their faith in God's word attacked by a professor they trusted.

Those brave enough to want to **defend** their Bible against any and all attacks. This is not a book. It is a "bullet." When you have a bullet you load your gun and do two things with it: You defend yourself...or go hunting. Good hunting!

Contents

Preface

The Reason for This Book

The original *Answer Book* was written in 1989. Over 50,000 of them are now in print and it is still popular. It is used by pastors who wish to explain to their people why our English Bible is perfect. It is used by college students who find their perfect Bible assailed in the classroom. It is used by average Christians who get tired of having their faith that God could, and did, preserve His word belittled and ridiculed by those of less faith.

In print for over 30 years *The Answer Book* has been studied by those who hate the King James Bible, **but they have never refuted it**. That is because it is founded on the principle that **the Bible is our Final Authority in ALL MATTERS of Faith and PRACTICE.**

So many arguments that were being used against the King James Bible for 30 years have been silenced by *The Answer Book* that anti-King James forces have had to turn to new ones. This book will do the same to those claims.

Question #63

Question: Where should a Bible believer begin when defending the Bible with a Bible corrector?

Answer: It is absolutely essential to begin by asking the Bible corrector this question, "Do you accept the Bible as your **Final Authority** in **all matters** of faith and **practice?**"

Explanation: Many times a Bible believer is challenged by someone who has many years of study in the area of Greek, Hebrew or textual criticism. Because their opponent has such an educational background the Bible believer is sometimes intimidated. In fact, most Bible correctors are quick to claim educational superiority if they think it will assist them in winning a debate.

Obviously, there are two answers to the question, "Do you accept the Bible as your **Final Authority** in **all matters** of faith and **practice?**" Yes, or No?

If the well-educated Bible corrector says, "Yes," they have just stated that they put the Bible **above** their own education. That puts them on an **equal level** with any Bible believer who may lack their educational credentials. Most Bible believers know their Bible better than the average Bible corrector, thus giving them the true advantage.

If, at anytime during the debate, the Bible corrector tries to pull rank on them by referring back to their educational "qualifications" the Bible believer needs only remind them, "But you said you accepted the Bible as your **Final Authority**, even above your education." This is devastating to both the argument and ego of heady Bible correctors.

On the other hand, if when asked this question they respond with "No,"...the Bible believer has already won the engagement and need go no further!

Question #64

Question: I've been told that we shouldn't make an issue out of Bible translations. Is that correct?

Answer: Not at all.

Explanation: Whenever someone comes up with this lame reasoning it is usually someone who, down deep in their heart, doesn't believe the King James Bible is the perfect word of God and doesn't want to incur the negative reaction they'll get from friends and fellow preachers if they take a public stand for it.

The hypocrisy of this statement is laughable. Those who try to hide behind this lame rationale usually make an issue out of things that pale in importance to the conviction that the Bible is the perfect word of God. They make an issue out of something they get **out** of the Bible but **not** the Bible **from which they get their issues!**

Anti-King James Bible believers are very much like evolutionists. Because they think they're right, they are usually prideful and arrogant. Then, once they go toe-to-toe with a Bible believer who knows his stuff, they suddenly pretend that making an issue of Bible translations is trivial and beneath them...in other words, they got "thumped" and the cowards are trying to find a way to look noble while they duck the issue at hand.

QUESTION #64

Just a few of the things they will rightfully make an issue out of are:

1. Salvation by grace
2. The Blood Atonement of Jesus Christ
3. The Local Church
4. The Pre-millennial Return of Christ
5. The Virgin Birth
6. The Deity of Christ
7. The Value of the Local Church

These are biblically accurate and worthy issues. But then there are many, which may be important such as:

1. Partakers of the Lord's Supper
2. Divorce
3. Dress standards
4. "Secondary Separation"
5. The Christian's diet
6. Is the earth is flat
7. What restaurants to eat at
8. The Head of the Home

Please understand. **All** of these may be deemed important enough to promote, teach, argue, break fellowship over, or make the subject of a sermon. Those who make these subjects an issue will say they do it because "the Bible says so!" **But**, the same people will suddenly go passive about making an issue out of the **Bible they claim they get these issues!** This reeks of all the sincerity of the indignation a politician shows when someone from the opposite party does something wrong but then is mute when someone from his own party does the same thing. Issues out of the Bible **can't supercede** the Bible those issues were taken from!

The Bible is used to establish many important truths:

1. Soul winning
2. Growth - It won't happen with new versions as well as with the AV

3. Historical teaching
4. Inspiration and encouragement
5. Warfare with the devil

Numbers **2** and **5** are extremely important to any Christian who wants to continue to improve their relationship with the Lord and wants to be a Defender of the Faith.

Question #65

Question: I've been told that the King James issue didn't start until 1950 and that it was started by Peter Ruckman. How can it be a genuine biblical issue then?

Answer: Simple, you were misinformed.

Explanation: Those who hate the preeminence of the King James Bible love to make the above claim. They denigrate the reputation of Dr. Peter S. Ruckman and then attempt to make the King James Issue an insignificant distraction begun by him. This simply isn't so.

I have personally wondered when militant advocates of the Perfect Bible became a visible entity in Christianity. Although I couldn't find a date or an occurrence that seemed to trigger the issue, my guess for a date of origin would have been sometime just after the Revised Version was published in 1884. My reasoning was that the RV was the first officially commissioned translation that was meant to replace the King James Bible. There were many insignificant independent translations from both the Textus Receptus and the Alexandrian Text prior to the RV but none had any official backing while the RV was commissioned by the Anglican Church as an English translation that was to replace the Authorized Version. (It failed miserably)

Then one day I was reading a book published in 1820. The title is *The Excellence of the Authorized Version of the*

Sacred Scriptures Defended Against the Socinians. It was published in 1820 and was the work of James Lister, of the Gloucester Street Chapel, Liverpool, England. In this work Rev. Lister was defending the King James Bible against a new version published by the "Socinians," the Unitarians. Although an apologist for the King James, Lister **did not** believe that it was absolutely perfect. This position makes two passing comments in the book utterly remarkable, for he makes two statements that **confirm** that there were those who believed the King James Bible was the **perfect word of God in his day.**

On page 16, while defending the Authorized Version against his Unitarian opponents he states, "...commentators as are known to be hostile to *new* versions, and wedded to the blemishes of our authorized translation." Thus, although he himself believed (wrongly) that the Authorized Version had errors in it, he plainly states that some in his day believed that what he called "blemishes" were not imperfections at all and that the AV did not need to be corrected or replaced.

Then on page 20, Lister refers to a Dr. Campbell who also did not believe the King James Bible to be perfect and was making excuse for those who altered it. Of Campbell, Lister says, "He is defending the utility of various translations, against those who oppose all innovation, and who seem to consider our present version as Infallible."

That is a profound revelation! It documents that all the way back in 1820 that there were those who believed the King James Bible was perfect and should not be altered in any way, who were "Ruckmanites" a hundred years before Ruckman was born and 130 years before the false date given by today's critics of that divine Book!

Question #66

Question: Didn't Peter Ruckman say that you can correct the Originals with the King James Bible?

Answer: Nope.

Explanation: The late Dr. Peter S. Ruckman weathered numerous attacks for his defense of the King James Bible. King James Bible haters and even many who embrace it love disparaging his character hoping to negate his defense of the King James Bible. One of their favorites is the above charge. Whenever you hear this **you will never hear it documented.** They will never show you in writing where he said it. Would **you** want to be so "quoted?" (Like Adam Schiff "quoted" President Trump's Ukranian phone call!)

Here is what Ruckman **actually** said, "We candidly and publicly confess that the King James text of the Old Testament is far superior to Kittel's Hebrew text, DeRossi's Hebrew text, Kennicott's Hebrew text or any Hebrew text that any of you are reading. We do not hesitate to state bluntly and openly that the King James text of the New Testament is superior to Erasmus' Greek text, Aland's Greek text, Metzger's Greek text, and any other that you are reading (or will read in the future.")[1]

---

1. Peter S. Ruckman, *Problem Texts*, (Pensacola Bible Institute Press), 1980, pg xii

He never mentioned the Originals, just the flawed texts that we have today. No one claims that **they** are word perfect.

Question #67

Question: Who started the King James Bible Issue?

Answer: There is no "King James Issue," it's a "Perfect Bible Issue."

Explanation: The people aligned against the King James Bible **do not** take that position for any of the reasons that they claim. It's not about manuscripts, proper translation, or archaic English words. It's about the one thing that absolutely terrifies them. It's the thought that there is a **perfect, flawless, Bible on this planet right now!** Why? Because if there **is** a perfect Bible in existence then we will all be judged by what we did with it. But if **no version out there is perfect then it's all a matter of personal preference as to which one you use.**

No one makes a claim of perfection for any of the modern versions on sale today. Only the King James Bible proponents are so bold and confident. That is why the King James is hounded so unfairly by those who fear it.

If today, we King James Bible believers declared that it **actually did** indeed have flaws in it, its many antagonists would rejoice that we finally admitted it. But then if we said, "Yep, the King James Bible isn't the perfect word of God...the **English Standard Version** is the perfect, inerrant word of God!" Everyone who is Anti-King James today would be Anti-English Standard Version tomorrow. Why?

Because the threat that a perfect Bible induces would still exist.

Question #68

Question: Is it necessary that we have a perfect, infallible Bible?

Answer: Absolutely.

Explanation: Those who publicly trumpet their love for the Bible but tuck their tails when asked if it's without error try to justify their infidelity to the Bible with statements like, "The Bible is accurate in doctrinal teaching." Or, "Although it has a few errors, it's still a reliable source for spiritual guidance."

For an example of this infidelity to the word of God, here is a portion of a note from the New Scofield Version found in 1 Chronicles 11:11: "God gave us a Bible free from error in the original manuscripts. In its preservation through many generations of recopying, He providentially kept it from any **serious error**, although He permitted a few **scribal mistakes**." (Emphasis mine)

What is humorous about this lame "defense" is that those making it have complete faith in the Bible's infallibility in matters that interest them, but hedge when prodded by a non-believer about perceived contradictions in the Bible.

If you believe there are "a few scribal mistakes" in the Bible, I have one question for you. **How many holes will you accept in your boat?**

Question #69

Question: If the Bible is "settled in Heaven," why should we make an issue of it here?

Answer: Because "here" is where it is being attacked.

Explanation: Many men who either don't truly believe the Bible is absolutely perfect, or, who are frightened at the thought of damage they will suffer if they defend it, like to present their cowardice as though it were a virtue. They boldly stick their chin out and quote, For ever, O Lord, thy word is settled in heaven. (Ps 119:89) like they wrote it themselves and declare that there is therefore no reason to make a fuss over the Bible down here.

I do not deny that there is probably a copy of the Bible in Heaven. But that Bible in Heaven isn't doing anything for us when atheists, agnostics and textual critics attack the validity of the Bible that **we carry, read and preach from.** No one is attacking the veracity of a Bible that's safely tucked away in Heaven. But they are carrying on a full force assault on the one in your hand. Therefore, it is an issue here.

Question #70

Question: Concerning getting involved in the Bible controversy I heard a preacher declare, "Defend the Bible? I'd rather defend a hungry lion!" That's a good stand to take, isn't it?

Answer: No. That isn't a "stand." It's a cop-out used to disguise either cowardice, ignorance or infidelity to the Bible.

Explanation: It seems that some men believe that you can get away with any stupid statement if you'll just say it boldly enough. This is one of those statements. To prove my point that **we do** need to defend the Bible I will sometimes place my Bible on the pulpit while preaching and say, "Hey Bible, you're a stupid book! You're powerless. Come on, Bible, why don't you do something about what I just said!" (Please forgive those remarks. I most certainly don't believe any of them but say them to make my point.) Of course my Bible does nothing. Why? Because it can't. It's a **book** and no book, even the one inspired by God can jump off a pulpit and defend itself.

I once read about a Columbian drug dealer who, when he wanted to smoke his marijuana would tear a page out of a Bible and roll his joint and smoke it. Why didn't the Bible stop him? You already know the answer.

Thus, we **must** defend the Bible not only against the heathen who so hate it but also against brethren who don't truly believe it and seek to destroy the faith that God's people have in it. But then, to do this defense would take away a good bit of the time used for practicing one's golf stroke. Furthermore, there are a great many who would lose friends and sacrifice opportunities if they bravely stand for the Bible. For most, that is just too high a price to pay for defending **GOD"S HOLY BIBLE!** It's much easier to play it safe: feign faithfulness, and tell any who question your inaction, "Defend the Bible? I'd rather defend a hungry lion!" Yeah, right!

Question #71

Question: Which "1611" do you use, the 1611, 1638 or 1769?

Answer: They're all the same Bible so it makes no difference.

Explanation: The first sale of a King James Bible is recorded to have taken place in May of 1611. Until September 2, 1752 the world operated on the Julian calendar which began the year on April 1. After that date it has followed the Gregorian calendar which begins the year on January 1. Thus, the "Good Ole 1611" was almost the "Good Ole 1610!"

The original 1611 had two unfortunate typesetting nuances. First was the fact that early Modern English had spelling that was not standardized. In fact, the word "said" can be found spelled four different ways in one single edition of the 1611 Authorized Version. In Gen 48:18 it is spelled: "saide"; Gen. 48:19, "said"; Judges 19:8, "sayd" and in 1 Sam 15:15 it is spelled "sayde." Understand, these are not spelling **errors**. It is simply a fact that spelling had not yet been standardized by 1611. (Nor for many years after.)

If you look at a facsimile of a 1611 you'll see these spelling abnormalities. Also, words like "son" were spelled "sonne," "evil" was "eville," "been" would sometimes be spelled "bene," "years" could be "yeeres," and "ye" could be spelled with one e or two. (In

Ezra 8:29 it is spelled both ways in the same verse.)

You can see why standardizing spelling would be a priority as reprints became necessary. These spelling issues were dealt with in later editions. They were **editions**, not **revisions**. An edition is an unchanged reprint of a book that is already in print. A revision is when the **text** of a book already in print **is changed** before reprinting. There have been no revisions of the King James Bible although there have been numerous editions. (King James Bible critics like to refer to the editions of the AV as revisions so they can claim modern translations are **also** a revision in a long line of revisions. Like all politics, honesty and accuracy never enter the equation.)

The most prominent editions of the King James Bible took place in 1638, 1762 and 1769 which is why these dates are bandied about in the infamous question, "Which King James Bible do you use...?"

Along with standardizing spelling there were also some spelling and printing errors that needed to be filtered out. These were handled with each succeeding edition.

The second shackle worn by the original King James Bibles was the font that was used. The font was Gothic which today can be found under the name "**Old English**." Because of this very title many today errantly believe the King James Bible was printed in **the language** of Old English when, in fact, it is Modern English, "thee's" and "thou's" withstanding.

The most popular font in use today is Times Roman, in which this and most books are typeset. There is no reason given why Robert Barker, the king's printer, chose the difficult-to-read Gothic font . The Geneva Bible, that preceded the King James by 50 years was typeset in the easier to read Times Roman, so we know it was in use in 1611.

Thus all those revisions of the King James Bible are actually **the same book** reprinted time and time again with necessary changes made to clarify the text.

At this time if you would like to protest, "Gipp is a King James Bible defender so that prejudices his data! I **still say** they were revisions and that so many revisions mean there are many different King James Bibles in print and they all read differently." (Don't worry, you can freely make this claim because people who hate the King James Bible will happily accept it and **never** check your facts.)

So, let's see if you **really** have a sincere problem with a bible being revised and printed which reads differently from one of the same name that was previously printed.

1. The New King James Bible - The NKJV was marketed as though it was a King James Bible edition without the "thee's" and "thou's." This simply isn't so. I've read the NKJV cover-to-cover four times and wrote a tract that reveals the serious flaws and mistranslations found within it. For this study we need only one reference to prove the difference between a revision and an edition.

The NKJV, first published in 1982, was **revised**, not edited, and republished in 1994. Why do I call it a revision rather than an edition? As stated above, it alters the wording of the original NKJV. It wasn't intended to correct printing errors. A comparison between the two proves this.

In Zechariah 13:6 is found a **prophetic reference** to the future crucifixion of Christ. It says,

And one shall say unto him, What are these wounds in thine hands?...

The NKJV of 1982 reads, And one will say to him, What are these wounds in your hands?... The word "thine" has been changed to "your" but it is obvious that the prophecy is still retained.

But, the 1994 revision was slipped in without informing potential readers (and customers) that **it didn't read the same** as the 1982 original. When you check Zech. 13 :6 in the 1994 revision you find that the prophecy has been eradicated by the revisors. And one will say to him, What are these wounds between your arms?... The reader can **plainly see** that the text has been changed and the prophecy destroyed in the revised version. No **honest** person can pretend to believe these two readings found **in the same version** are not different. (All of the popular conservative modern versions; the ASV, NASV, NIV, ESV, etc., also eliminate this prophecy.)

You will not find such changes between the various **editions** of the King James Bible.

If you use (and defend?) the corrupted NKJV version, may I ask you a question? Which New King James Version do you use, the 1982 or the 1994?

2. The New American Standard Version - You want editions and revisions? Get an NASV! Originally published in 1960 there are also editions printed in 1962, 1963, 1968, 1971, 1975, 1977 and 1995. Ironically the 1995 NASV is called the "Reader's Edition." It must be embarrassing for the publishers to have to admit that the earlier editions were hard to read! This is not a vain charge made by a KJV only guy. That the NASV is stilted and rough and hard to read has long been known and was **obviously** a factor in the printing of the 1995 revision.

But not all NASV's are created equal. The NASV is a translation of the flawed 23rd Edition of the Nestle-Aland Greek New Testament. One of the many errors found in this Greek New Testament was the blatant omission of the ascension of Jesus Christ attested to in Luke 24:51 where it declares, And it came to pass, while he blessed them, he was parted from them, and carried up into heaven.

But those words, "...and carried up into heaven" didn't sit well with the Nestle-Aland editors so they removed them and the resulting marred NASV read, And it came about that while He was blessing them, He parted from them.

Again, no **honest** person can write this off to a mere edition. Not only does every NASV from 1960 to 1977 omit the ascension of Jesus Christ in Luke 24:51 but they also delete the worship the Apostles paid him in the next verse! Where the Bible says, And they worshipped him, and returned to Jerusalem with great joy: the NASV lamely states, And they returned to Jerusalem with great joy,

But while making the NASV "readable" in 1995, the word-smiths reinstated Christ's ascension. (I'm sure there was "joy in Heaven!") The 1995 **revision** of the old NASV reads thus in both verses: **51** While He was blessing them, He parted from them and was carried up into heaven.
52 And they, after worshiping Him, returned to Jerusalem with great joy,

Again, it cannot be denied that these are two entirely different readings that are found in the "same" (except for all the alterations) bibles!

Hey! Do you use a New American Standard Version? Which NASV do you use, a 1960, 1962, 1963, 1968, 1971, 1975, 1977 or a 1995?

3. The New International Version - The original NIV was first published in 1973 with new editions coming out in 1978, 1984 and 2011. Yet, they don't all read the same.

In Luke 16:23 the Bible says, And in hell he lift up his eyes, being in torments, and seeth Abraham afar off, and Lazarus in his bosom. in reference to the eternal destiny of the rich man in the famous historical account of the Rich Man & Lazarus.

While most modern versions replace the word "hell" with "hades" the NIV of 1973 stuck with the tried & true "hell"...until its later revisions. The editions of the NIV that preceded the 2001 revision also read, In hell he... but with the 2011 "hell" was expunged. All NIV's printed since 2011 read, In Hades, where he was.. If you say they are the same go look in a mirror and you'll see a dishonest person staring back at you! So, which NIV do you use, the 1973, 1978, 1984 or the 2011?

4. The Holman Christian Standard Bible - This modern version takes the practice of making changes to a new heights. (or depth). When it was first published in 1999 it **wasn't** the Holman Christian Standard Bible at all. It was published as the Holman Christian **Study** Bible. Somewhere along the long line of revisions from 1999 to 2000, to 2002, 2003 and 2009 the "Study" was dropped in favor of "Standard." That is almost humorous. A "standard" is **STANDARD!** But the meaning of the letters HCSB aren't even "standard." They change with time. So what do you use, a Holman Christian **Study** Bible or a Holman Christian **Standard** Bible?

5. The Living Bible - I blush to reveal this to you but in the name of honesty I am required to do so. It is said that Kenneth Taylor, the creator of the Living Bible took the American Standard Version and wrote it in a simple format so his children could understand it. Well, okay, if you say so.

When the Living Bible was first marketed in 1971 it included a vulgar but common phrase when in 1 Samuel 20:30 Saul angrily confronts his son Jonathan over his loyalty to young David. In the Bible this verse reads, Then Saul's anger was kindled against Jonathan, and he said unto him, Thou son of the perverse rebellious woman, do not I know that thou hast chosen the son of Jesse to thine own confusion, and unto the confusion of thy mother's nakedness?

Instead of saying, "perverse rebellious woman" the original Living Bible said, "You son of a b—h!" Yes, that is the truth. I knew of a preacher who went to a Christian bookstore, opened a Living Bible to that section and read it out loud for all to hear. The manager came over and told him he couldn't use that kind of language in his Christian establishment. The Preacher said, "I'm not using it. I'm just reading out loud from a bible that **you** sell!"

The latest revision of the Living Bible, the New Living Translation of 2015, puts it this way, You stupid son of a whore! (Very uplifting!)

So, if you use a Living Bible of some kind, which do you use, an SOB or SOW version?

As you can see, critics of the King James Bible are very much like Congressional Democrats that rage about the "crimes" of Conservatives but are stone silent when they do the very same thing. If you wish to join such hypocrites simply challenge King James Bible users with the smug retort, "Which King James do you use, the 1611, 1638 or 1769?" and forget you ever read this. Who knows? Get good enough at your hypocrisy and you may end up in Congress!

Question #72

Question: Why do King James Bible believers refuse to accept the Greek New Testament manuscripts from Alexandria as superior to those from Antioch?

Answer: Because King James Bible believers are more biblical than those who embrace the corrupt manuscripts from Alexandria, Egypt.

Explanation: The question asked here ought to be, "Why would anyone who believes the Bible **ever** believe that Alexandria, Egypt, would be the location the Lord would use to preserve his Bible?" Any honest student of Scripture cannot but admit that the predominant view of Egypt throughout the Bible is negative. Examine these references and you will find the truth about Egypt:

1. Gen. 12:10-12 - First Mention is negative
2. Gen 37:36 - Joseph is made a slave in Egypt
3. Ex 1:11 - Israel became slaves in Egypt
4. Ex 1:16 - Pharaoh told the Jewish midwives to murder all male Jewish babies
5. Ex. 20:2 God calls it a "house of bondage"
6. Deu. 17:16 - Commercial trade is forbidden with Egypt
7. 2 Chr. 36:2, 3 - Egypt is a perpetual enemy of Israel
8. Isa. 19:1 - God swore vengeance on the "idols of Egypt"
9. Isa. 30:2, 3 - Israel is commanded not to trust Egypt

10. Isa. 31:1 - Israel is told not to turn to Egypt for help
11. Jer. 42:18, 19 - God was angry with the Jews who went to Egypt for safety
12. Jer. 44:12, 27 - God says He would punish the Jews who went to Egypt for safety
13. Jer. 46:20-24 - God prophesies destruction on Egypt
14. Ezek. 29:2 - God prophesies destruction on Egypt
15. Ezek. 29:7-9 - Israel was defiled with the idols of Egypt
16. Ezek. 30:4, 13, 16,19 - God prophesies destruction on Egypt
17. Ezek. 32:15-18 - God prophesies destruction on Egypt
18. Dan. 11:42 - Prophecy of judgement against Egypt
19. Joel 3:19 - Prophecy of judgement against Egypt
20. Rev. 11:8 - God compares fallen Jerusalem to "Sodom and Egypt"

If the Bible is your "Final authority in **all matter** of faith and **practice**," why on earth, after viewing the above negative statements the Bible contains about Egypt, would you think for one second that Egypt is the location He would use to preserve His sacred Book?

Furthermore, there is no record in Scripture that God had any of His people go to Egypt in the early history of the Church as recorded in the book of Acts. Peter never visited Egypt. In three missionary trips the Apostle Paul never visited Egypt. Philip, the first martyr of the Church was murdered due to the contention that was started by people, some of whom were from Alexandria. (Acts 6:9)

In fact, what a true Bible believer should do is wonder why **academia** is so enamored with this unholy location. Why do they insist on turning their backs on the vast majority of

QUESTION #72

Greek New Testament manuscripts which come from Antioch, the center of New Testament Christianity and promote a handful of Greek manuscripts which **were never accepted or used** by the New Testament Church? In light of the Bible's testimony and the record of history **anyone** who exalts anything about Egypt is more likely to be viewed as a enemy of God and His Book than as a friend, no matter **what** your college Greek professor told you!

Question #73

Question: I believe and use only the King James Bible, no modern versions. But I don't claim it's perfect and, in fact, I sometimes use the Greek to correct it. Is that all right to do?

Answer: No. You're not actually correcting the King James Bible with the Greek. You are taking the **perfect** Bible and making it imperfect.

Explanation: If you use the King James Bible, you are probably aware that all Bibles originate from one of two locations, Antioch, Syria, and Alexandria, Egypt. The **vast majority** of the 5,800+ manuscripts of the Greek New Testament come from what is known as the Antiochan, or Traditional Text, most often referred to as the Textus Receptus. This is the Greek text used in the translation of the King James Bible. The second source for Greek manuscripts is known as the Critical Text and is a product of the corrupt manuscripts produced in Alexandria, Egypt. This text represents a handful of corrupt manuscripts yet they are the darlings of textual critics.

While many King James Bible proponents know that Antioch and Alexandria are the sources of two entirely different sets of Greek New Testament manuscripts, many are totally unaware that these two locations are also the origin of two opposing views of Scripture which define how we look at the Bible as a whole. Each location presents its own unique **mentality** through which the Bible is viewed.

The two items we get from Antioch are:

1. The **Antiochan Text** which is composed of the vast majority of manuscripts representing the pure text of the Bible.

2. The **Antiochan Mentality** which can be defined as: "The Bible is perfect and **cannot** be improved on." Those who espouse this mentality accept the King James Bible **as is** and make no effort to alter it in any way because they believe it cannot be made better than it is.

The two items we get from Alexandria are:

1. The **Alexandrian Text** which is composed of corrupted manuscripts of the Greek New Testament originating in Alexandria, Egypt.

2. A mentality that the Bible is not really perfect. In fact, the **Alexandrian Mentality** can be defined in this simple statement: "The Bible is **not** perfect and **can** be improved on." Those who embrace this mentality do not believe that **any** Bible is perfect no matter what version it is. Some use one or more of the modern versions sold at religious book stores. But, some of those who adhere to this mentality use and believe only the King James Bible. While they may use the King James Bible they **do not** believe that it is perfect and believe, like any Alexandrian, that the King James Bible can be improved on through the use of Greek and Hebrew study. This is an error. You only need to make one change to perfection to produce imperfection!

Probably when you were in Bible college a teacher convinced you that going to the Greek was a valid method of Bible study. It isn't. If anyone claims it is, then the simple question is: What do you do when **two different people** change the **same word** in the **same verse** but change it in a different manner? They can't agree on what's right but can only conclude that the Bible is wrong. Hence, "The Bible is **not** perfect and **can** be improved on."

All question of proper translation ended in 1611. When someone "goes to the Greek" they reopen a crisis which has been resolved for over 400 years. And all they have to offer is their **sanctified** opinion. Yet someone else looking at the same word and using the same Greek may say the Bible should be altered with a completely different rendering. Then, some other "expert" chimes in with his "divine" opinion. Soon, the only thing they can agree on is that "The Bible is **not** perfect and **can** be improved on." But, **none of them** can authoritatively decree what is correct! Once you remove the **final authority** from the Bible and bestow it on a sinner your Bible becomes a shipwreck at the mercy of the winds of a fallible human.

You are better served to simply accept the Perfect Bible as your final authority and ignore all the experts who are great at casting doubt on the word of God but can't find or produce a perfect copy of it.

Question #74

Question: Why won't Bible believers admit that their beloved Textus Receptus is based on late, inferior manuscripts?

Answer: Because it isn't.

Explanation: The charge that the Textus Receptus is based on late, inferior manuscripts is often leveled against the King James Bible. Unfortunately for those making the charge they are only wrong **twice**.

Although many of the manuscripts that make up the Textus Receptus are indeed late, some even having been produced after the King James Bible, this is not a factor in determining the original text of the New Testament. Very simply, if the text has already been established by ancient witnesses, then all that the great mass of later witnesses do is attest to the fact that it was the text of choice among New Testament Christians rather than that of Alexandria, Egypt.

Disputed passages found in the Textus Receptus and omitted from flawed modern versions have manuscript attestation from as early as the Second Century, such as Tatian's (150 AD) references to 1 John 5:7. Therefore, if the correct text was established well before 1611 Greek manuscripts produced after that date simply "Amen" the correct text but are simply "more bricks in the wall" which stands on the foundation revealed in the Second Century.

Therefore, the King James Bible is **not** based on inferior manuscripts but **superior** manuscripts. Which in fact preserve the very text of the Originals and which were used by the True Church since its inception.

Secondly, the manuscripts testifying to the original text as found in the King James Bible aren't inferior in either quality or textual value. I always laugh when a Bible rejector resorts to the lame defense of their corrupt modern version of, "Well, I can still find the doctrines in my modern version, to which I add, yes, the doctrine you learned **from a King James Bible!**

Question #75

Question: When was the New Testament canon finalized?

Answer: Amazingly the canon of the New Testament was sorted out and finalized within the first two centuries.

Explanation: There are a great number of witnesses to what was and was not accepted by the New Testament Church as the authentic, inspired writings of the New Testament. Below you will find the testimony of those witnesses.

The Canon of the New Testament

1. Marcion the Heretic, 85AD - 160AD: Although a heretic, Marcion still gave an accurate testimony to the canon of the New Testament. He acknowledged the authenticity of:

Luke
Galatians
1Corinthians
2 Corinthians
Romans
1 Thessalonians
2 Thessalonians
Ephesians
Colossians
Philemon
Philippians

2. Valentinus, 2nd - 3rd Century: Like Marcion, Valentinus was also a false teacher. But due to his heretical teachings, he forced the Church to clarify which books of the New Testament were authentic and which were not. He was a Gnostic who believed a series of outlandish doctrines concerning God, mankind and salvation. His teachings held their most influence between 136AD and 165AD in Rome and Alexandria. Valentinus and his followers verified the authenticity of:

Matthew	Galatians
Mark	Ephesians
Luke	Philippians
John	Colossians
Romans	1 Peter
1 Corinthians	1 John
2 Corinthians	The Revelation

3. Ignatius of Antioch, circa 35/50 - 108/110AD: Ignatius was the third bishop of the church in Antioch. He was contemporary with Polycarp, the bishop of Smyrna. In fact, it is claimed that both he and Polycarp were students of the Apostle John. Although he never refers to any of the books of the New Testament by name, he pointedly quotes from the following:

Matthew	1 Corinthians
Luke	Ephesians
Acts	Colossians
Romans	1 Thessalonians

4. Polycarp of Smyrna, 70AD - 155AD: Polycarp bridges the gap from the Apostles to the Church in history. As Ignatius he was said to have been a disciple of the Apostle John and it is claimed that it was John who ordained him bishop of the church at Smyrna. Only one work of Polycarp has survived, his *Letter to the Philippians*, and it is this link to the Apostolic age that sheds such amazing light on the Canon of Scripture. In this work Polycarp refers to seventeen of the twenty-seven books that make up the New Testament. He makes reference to:

Matthew	1 Thessalonians
Mark	2 Thessalonians
Luke	1 Timothy
Acts	2 Timothy
1 Corinthians	Hebrews
2 Corinthians	1 Peter
Galatians	1 John
Ephesians	3 John
Philippians	

5. Justin Martyr, 100AD - 165AD: Justin was a Gentile philosopher who turned to Christ when he recognized philosophy's inability to answer the questions of life. His testimony concerning which books then circulating the Christian world were authentic is helpful in picking the four authentic gospels out of the sea of frauds. He also testifies to the authenticity of John's Revelation. He makes positive references to:

Matthew	Philippians
Mark	Colossians
Luke	2 Thessalonians
John	1 Timothy
Romans	Titus
1 Corinthians	Hebrews
Galatians	1 John
Ephesians	Revelation

6. Irenaeus of Lyons, 115/140AD - 200/203: Irenaeus was a Second Century Christian leader and the bishop of the church in a part of Gaul that is now Lyons, France. It is speculated that when Polycarp went to Rome to argue in favor of a scriptural rather than pagan dating for Easter that Irenaeus accompanied him. Concerning the Canon, he was the first to testify to the authenticity of only the four Gospels we have in our Bible today, disqualifying any others. He also makes reference to other writings that are believed to be Hebrews, James and 2 Peter without mentioning them by name. He quoted from every New Testament book except: Philemon, 2 Peter, 3 John, and Jude. Thus he vouched for the authenticity of:

Matthew	Galatians	Titus
Mark	Ephesians	Hebrews
Luke	Philippians	James
John	Colossians	1 Peter
Acts	1 Thessalonians	2 Peter
Romans	2 Thessalonians	1 John
1 Corinthians	1 Timothy	2 John
2 Corinthians	2 Timothy	Revelation

7. Quintus Septimius Florens Tertullianus, 155/160 - 220?AD: Tertullian was born into a pagan family in Carthage in northern Africa in present day Tunisia. Having received an excellent education in Carthage, he journeyed to Rome in his late teens or early twenties possibly to study law. While there he was impressed by the courage of the Christian martyrs he saw and was eventually converted to Christ. Concerning the Canon, Tertullian's published works give a solid testimony. While some question the authenticity of 2 Timothy & Titus, Tertullian defends them along with each of Paul's epistles and even chides Marcian for rejecting Titus and Paul's two epistles to Timothy. In his writings he quotes from every book of the New Testament with the exception of: 2 Peter, James, 2 John and 3 John. Thus, Tertullian's testimony authenticates:

Matthew	2 Corinthians	1 Timothy
Mark	Galatians	2 Timothy
Luke	Ephesians	Titus
John	Philippians	Philemon
Acts	Colossians	1 Peter
Romans	1 Thessalonians	1 John
1 Corinthians	2 Thessalonians	Revelation

8. Titus Flavius Clemens, 150AD - 211/215: It is believed that Clement of Alexandria was born in Athens of pagan parents and moved to Alexandria in adulthood. He was thoroughly studied in Greek mythology and Hellenistic philosophy. He never broke free of these influences and they are interwoven through his writings. In spite of this, within his writings he quotes all the books of the New Testament except: Philemon, James, 2 Peter, 2 John and 3 John. Unfortunately he also quoted both Old and New Testament apocryphal writings. Of the true New Testament, he quoted:

Matthew	2 Corinthians	2 Timothy
Mark	Galatians	Titus
Luke	Ephesians	Hebrews
John	Philippians	1 Peter
Acts	Colossians	1 John
Romans	1 Thessalonians	Jude
1 Corinthians	2 Thessalonians	Revelation
	1 Timothy	

9. Origen Adamantius, 185- 254AD: Origen was born and raised in Alexandria, Egypt. He was a Platonic philosopher with some Aristotle and Stoicism mixed in. He never abandoned philosophy and superimposed it over his view of the Bible. Origen did not believe in the redemptive payment for sins that Jesus Christ made. He taught it was merely a martyr's sacrifice in order to make a statement for the general good. He thought salvation was obtained by following the example of the Logos. He didn't believe in a literal Hell or in the physical resurrection of Christ. He did not believe in the triune Godhead. He looked at Scripture for an allegorical teaching rather than a literal one. But, within his vast quantity of writings he quoted 24 of the 27 New Testament books, 2 Peter, 2 John and 3 John being excluded. Thus, in spite of his many doctrinal errors he verifies the authenticity of:

Matthew	Galatians	Titus
Mark	Ephesians	Philemon
Luke	Philippians	Hebrews
John	Colossians	James
Acts	1 Thessalonians	1 Peter
Romans	2 Thessalonians	1 John
1 Corinthians	1 Timothy	Jude
2 Corinthians	2 Timothy	Revelation

10. Athanasius 296-373AD: Athanasius was another of the early Church Fathers. He stood against the Arians in his defense of the Trinitarianism doctrine of the Godhead. Among Athanasius' writings is one entitled the *Thirty-Ninth Festal Epistle,* which he wrote in 367AD. In this epistle Athanasius deals directly with the issue of the canon of Scripture and lists the canonical books of both the Old and

New Testaments. He calls them "the wells of salvation, so that he who thirsts may be satisfied with the sayings in these. Let no one add to these. Let nothing be taken away." Athanasius made it plain that he was dealing directly with the issue of which extant books were authentic and which were fraudulent. He derided the apocryphal writings and **defined the New Testament Canon as the twenty-seven books we now have.** With the testimony of Athanasius we find all twenty-seven books of the New Testament authenticated and the apocryphal writings officially excluded from Scripture.

11. The Muratorian Canon, 200AD: Ludovico Antonio Muratori (1672 - 1750) was an Italian historian and was a leading scholar of his day. Muratori's passion was the publication of ancient texts so they would not disappear into the mists of history. While perusing the Ambrosian Library in Milan he came upon an amazing discovery and one that would have an impact on a 21st century Bible believer. He discovered an 8th century Latin manuscript which was found to be a catalog of the books accepted as authentic by the early Church. This catalog was published around 200 AD. Furthermore, it has been determined that it was a Latin translation of an earlier Greek manuscript. That means the canon of Scripture found within it was that which was accepted by the **First Century Church!** Muratori published the manuscript in 1740 and it has since been referred to as the Muratorian Canon. An additional four fragments of the 11th and 12th centuries of the manuscript were later found in Montecassino in 1897. The first portion of the manuscript is missing as is the ending. But that which is preserved sheds great light on the condition of the canon in the second century. In this manuscript the Gospel of Luke is referred to as "the third Gospel book" leaving place for Matthew and Mark in the missing first portion. The Muratorian Canon refers to two epistles written by the Apostle John, but doesn't say which of the three they are.

The Muratorian Canon authenticates:

Gospel #1	2 Corinthians	2 Timothy
Gospel #2	Galatians	Titus
Luke	Ephesians	1 John (?)
John	Philippians	2 John (?)
Acts	Colossians	Jude
Romans	1 Thessalonians	Revelation
1 Corinthians	2 Thessalonians	

Thus the Muratorian Canon verifies the authenticity of eighteen of our New Testament books directly, although not specifying which of John's epistles it refers to and gives a silent nod to two gospels appearing ahead of the third, Luke, which can only refer to Matthew and Mark since no other "gospel" made this claim. Any testimony concerning the remainder of the catholic Epistles has disappeared with the lost closing pages of the work.

Question #76

Question: I've been told that we should avoid modern versions translated by liberal scholars but that those translated by conservative scholars are trustworthy. Is this correct to do?

Answer: No. None of them can be trusted.

Explanation: First, let me say that no one should offhandedly simply accept a statement of an "expert." They should question it and look into it. People accept "expert testimonies" because they lack the time to do their own thorough study of the subject or simply because they're too lazy to investigate a subject on their own. I admit that you cannot dedicate your life to every area of knowledge, but there are some statements that can be easily checked out.

Concerning this statement about liberal translations being untrustworthy while conservative translations are trustworthy, there is a very simple way to establish whether it is a valid rule to follow. Why not check verses in the Bible that liberal translations corrupt and see how the conservative translations handle the same important verses?

As to defining whether we consign a version to either the liberal or conservative category we will do it as follows:

Liberal Translations

1. New Living Translation - NLT
2. Revised Version of 1885 - RV
3. Revised Standard Version - RSV

4. New Revised Standard Version - NRSV
5. Holman Christian Standard Bible - HCSB

Conservative Translations
1. New King James Version[2] - NKJV
2. Modern English Version - MEV
3. American Standard Version - ASV
4. New American Standard Version77 - NASV77
5. New American Standard Version95 - NASV95
6. New International Version - NIV
7. English Standard Version - ESV

Genesis 22:8

Problem: This verse prophesies that God will provide **"Himself** a lamb" for the sacrifice needed. Although the subject here is Abraham's willingness to obey God, there is a greater picture of God the Father (Abraham, in type) who is willing to sacrifice His Son (Isaac, in type) for the sacrifice needed. But this is more than just a typological view. It **must** have a future reference to the Cross of Calvary because, even though Abraham is told that God will provide himself a lamb for the sacrifice needed God never gave Abraham a **lamb**. He got a **ram.** The "Lamb," Jesus Christ, God in the flesh, didn't show up for almost two thousand years! But this prophecy is obliterated in almost every modern translation, as you will see below.

---

2. Please note that both the New King James Version and the Modern English Version are translated from the Antiochan Text just as the King James Bible is. The others all use the corrupt Alexandrian Text from Egypt.

QUESTION #76

KJB - And Abraham said, My son, God will provide himself a lamb for a burnt offering: so they went both of them together.
RV - God will provide himself the lamb
ASV - God will provide himself the lamb
RSV - God will provide himself the lamb
NASV77 - God will provide for Himself
NIV - God himself will provide
NKJV - God will provide for Himself
NASV95 - God will provide for Himself
NRSV - God himself will provide
NLT - God will provide a sheep
HCSB - God Himself will provide
ESV - God will provide for himself
MEV - God will provide for Himself

Correct: RV, RSV, ASV,
Conservatives: 1
Liberals: 2
Corrupted: NASV77, NIV, NKJV, NASV95, NRSV, NLT, HCSB, ESV, MEV
Conservatives: 6
Liberals: 3
Conclusion: Six out of seven "conservative" translations corrupt the verse along with most of the liberal translations. In fact, twice as many liberal translations preserve this truth correctly as so-called "conservative" translations.

1 Samuel 13:1
Problem: Anyone who can read can plainly see that by the end of verse one Saul has ben king over Israel for two years. Yet, somehow this seems to grate at the hearts of scholarship

for almost all of them have altered the verse by adding some variation of years to the verse. Other than the NKJV none of the modern versions, conservative or liberal get the verse completely right. The amazing thing about these scriptural train wrecks is that they will all admit, sometimes in a footnote, that there is **no Hebrew authority** for the numbers that they arbitrarily insert into the text. **They made them up!** Thus, while they cannot agree on what is **correct** they all agree on the one main rule that all modern translators follow, "The King James Bible is **always** wrong."

KJB - Saul **reigned one year; and when he had reigned two years** over Israel,
RV - Saul was **thirty years old** when he began to reign; and he reigned two years over Israel.
ASV - Saul was **forty years old** when he began to reign; and when he had reigned two years over Israel,
RSV - Saul was **... years old** when he began to reign; and he reigned **...** and two years over Israel.
NASV77 - Saul was **forty years old** when he began to reign, and he reigned **thirty-two years** over Israel.
NIV - Saul was **thirty years old** when he became king, and he reigned over Israel **forty-two years.**
NKJV - Saul reigned one year; and when he had reigned two years over Israel,
NASV95 - Saul was **thirty years old** when he began to reign, and he reigned **forty two years** over Israel.
NRSV - Saul was **... years old** when he began to reign; and he reigned **...** and two years over Israel.
NLT - Saul was **thirty years old** when he became king, and he reigned for **forty-two years.**

QUESTION #76

HCSB - Saul was **30 years old** when he became king, and he reigned **42 years over** Israel.
ESV - Saul lived for one year and then became king, and when he had reigned for two years over Israel,
MEV - Saul was **thirty years old** when he began to reign, and he reigned **forty-two years over** Israel.

Correct: NKJV
Conservatives: 1
Liberals: 0
Corrupted: RV, ASV, RSV, NASV77, NIV, NASV95, NRSV, NLT, HCSB, ESV, MEV
Conservatives: 6
Liberals: 5
Conclusion: Only the NKJV preserves the correct reading. In fact, more "conservative" translations sabotage the correct reading than do liberals. There is certainly no advantage by blindly accepting that a "conservative" translation is going to be in some way superior to one savaged by liberals.

2 Samuel 21:19
Problem: As stated elsewhere in this work, by removing the italicized words, *the brother of* modern translations, conservative or liberal, introduce not one but **two** contradictions that simply are not there in God's perfect Bible. These uncalled for alterations record David killing Goliath in **1 Sam. 17:50** while they later claim that Elhanan killed Goliath in **2 Sam. 21:19**. Then because they claim Elhanan killed Goliath in 2 Sam there is then a contradiction with **1 Chr. 20:5** where **they all say** Elhanan actually killed Lahmi, **the brother of** Goliath. One alteration of the truth

nets two contradictions! We call that "Economy of Corruption!"

KJB - And there was again a battle in Gob with the Philistines, where Elhanan the son of Jaareoregim, a Bethlehemite, ***slew the brother of*** Goliath the Gittite, the staff of whose spear was like a weaver's beam.

RV - slew Goliath

ASV - slew Goliath

RSV - slew Goliath

NASV77 - killed Goliath

NIV - killed the brother of Goliath

NKJV - killed *the brother of* Goliath

NASV95 - killed Goliath

NRSV - killed Goliath

NLT - killed the brother of Goliath

HCSB - killed Goliath

ESV - struck down Goliath

MEV - struck down Goliath

Correct: NIV, NKJV, NLT,

Conservatives: 2

Liberals: 1

Corrupted: RV, ASV, RSV, NASV77, NASV95, NRSV, HCSB, ESV, MEV

Conservatives: 5

Liberals: 4

Conclusion: Having been translated by conservative scholars does not guarantee that a modern version will not be free of man-induced contradictions.

QUESTION #76

Micah 5:2

Problem: Here we find another prophecy concerning Jesus Christ coming under attack. In Micah where it records the birthplace of Jesus Christ being Bethlehem it states that the One coming from there is from "everlasting" making the claim that He is also the eternal God. This statement concerning the deity of Christ is destroyed when modern translators render the verse to read "from ancient times", or something to that effect. This change makes Jesus Christ not eternal and not God in the flesh. While one liberal translation actually stayed true to the truth we find that two conservative translations destroyed the truth as readily as the majority of liberal translations.

KJB - But thou, Bethlehem Ephratah, though thou be little among the thousands of Judah, yet out of thee shall he come forth unto me that is to be ruler in Israel; whose goings forth have been from of old, **from everlasting.**

RV - from everlasting.

ASV - from everlasting.

RSV - from ancient days.

NASV77 - From the days of eternity.

NIV - from ancient times.

NKJV - From everlasting.

NASV95 - From the days of eternity.

NRSV - from ancient days.

NLT - from the distant past.

HCSB - from eternity.

ESV - from ancient days.

MEV - from ancient days.

Correct: RV, ASV, NIV, NASV77, NKJV, NASV95
Conservatives: 5
Liberals: 1
Corrupted: ESV, HCSB, RSV, NRSV, NLT, MEV
Conservatives: 2
Liberals: 4
Conclusion: Both the ESV and the MEV read in agreement with the majority of liberal translations. Buying a "conservative" translation isn't always a way to secure a Bible that is God-friendly.

Zechariah 13:6
Problem: It seems modern translators have a real resentment for Old Testament prophecies about Jesus Christ. You just saw what they did to a reference to Him being God in the flesh. Here they make an attack on a prophecy of how He would die. The words, "wounds in thine hands" plainly foreshadows the crucifixion of the Lord yet **not one** modern version preserves the prophecy. Everyone of these "bibles" is weaker than the splendid King James. (Other than the King James Bible I have only copied the first half of the verse since that is the portion pertaining to the prophecy.)
KJB - And one shall say unto him, **What are these wounds in thine hands?** Then he shall answer, Those with which I was wounded in the house of my friends.
RV - What are these wounds between thine arms?
ASV - What are these wounds between thine arms?
RSV - What are these wounds on your back?
NASV77 - What are these wounds between your arms?
NIV - What are these wounds on your body?
NKJV - What are these wounds between your arms?

QUESTION #76

NASV95 - What are these wounds between your arms?
NRSV - What are these wounds on your chest?
NLT - Then what about those wounds on your chest?
HCSB - What are these wounds on your chest?
ESV - What are these wounds on your back?
MEV - What are these wounds on your arms?

Correct: None
Conservatives: 0
Liberals: 0
Corrupted: RV, ASV, RSV, NASV77, NIV, NKJV, NASV95, NRSV, NLT, HCSB, ESV, MEV
Conservatives: 7
Liberals: 5
Conclusion: It is plain to see to anyone who is an objective thinker that being translated by conservative scholars didn't prevent Bible truth from being eliminated from the pages of scripture, and conservative scholars are no greater friend to the Bible than are their liberal brethren.

Matthew 18:11
Problem: Here we find a wonder truth...**that is totally missing from some** modern version! This **is not** an incidental verse! Yet its wonderful truth is attacked and removed from many liberal translations and even some which are labeled "conservative." While five of the conservative translations and one liberal translation have the verse in the text, two conservative translations join with four liberal translations in removing this great truth from the Bible.
KJB - For the Son of man is come to save that which was lost.
In: ASV, NASV77, NKJV, NASV95, HCSB, MEV

Conservatives: 5
Liberals: 1
Removed: RV, RSV, NIV, NRSV, NLT, ESV
Conservatives: 2
Liberals: 4
Conclusion: Here having a conservative translation helps, if you buy **the right** conservative translation. But buying a conservative translation is not a "sure thing" for getting the truth.

Mark 1:2
Problem: Many modern versions change "the prophets" to read "Isaiah the prophet" thus **inserting a contradiction where there is none** since the quotes come from two prophets, Isaiah and Malachi, not Isaiah alone.
KJB - As it is written **in the prophets**, Behold, I send my messenger before thy face, which shall prepare thy way before thee.

RV - Isaiah the prophet
ASV - Isaiah the prophet
RSV - Isaiah the prophet
NASV77 - Isaiah the prophet
NIV - Isaiah the prophet
NKJV - the Prophets
NASV95 - Isaiah the prophet
NRSV - the prophet Isaiah
NLT - the prophet Isaiah
HCSB - Isaiah the prophet
ESV - Isaiah the prophet
MEV - the Prophets

Correct: NKJV, MEV
Conservatives: 2
Liberals: 0
Corrupted: RV, ASV, RSV, NASV77, NIV, NASV95, NRSV, NLT, HCSB, ESV
Conservatives: 5

QUESTION #76

Liberals: 5

Conclusion: Only two so-called conservative translations are free of this error. The other five read exactly like the liberal translations.

Luke 16:23

Problem: The simple Bible truth of "hell" seems to uniformly upset **all** translators since **all** modern versions join forces in eliminating it from their pages.

KJB - And in **hell** he lift up his eyes, being in torments, and seeth Abraham afar off, and Lazarus in his bosom.

RV - Hades
ASV - Hades
RSV - Hades
NASV77 - Hades
NIV - Hades
NKJV - Hades
NASV95 - Hades
NRSV - Hades
NLT - the place of the dead
HCSB - Hades
ESV - Hades
MEV - Hades

Correct: None
Conservatives: 0
Liberals:)
Corrupted: RV, ASV, RSV, NASV77, NIV, NKJV, NASV95, NRSV, NLT, HCSB, ESV, MEV
Conservatives: 7
Liberals: 5

Conclusion: Once again, the "conservative/liberal" argument falls apart in this representation of basic, simple biblical truth. There is a place of eternal torment. It is fire. For thousands of years it has been referred to as "Hell." Yet even this simple Bible truth comes under attack when placed in the care of **scholarship**, be it conservative or liberal. Go ahead Preacher, use your "conservative" translation next week to preach about the "Rich Man in Hades." I'll bet it strikes terror into the hearts of your listeners.

Luke 23:33

Problem: This is the only single verse in the Bible where the word "Calvary" is found. Yet this precious place that we love to sing about has been banished from all liberal translations and the vast majority of those foisted on Christianity as "conservative."

KJB - And when they were come to the place, which is called Calvary, there they crucified him, and the malefactors, one on the right hand, and the other on the left.

RV - The skull
ASV - The skull
RSV - The skull
NASV77 - The skull
NIV - the skull
NKJV - Calvary
NASV95 - The skull
NRSV - The skull
NLT - The skull
HCSB - The skull
ESV - The skull
MEV - The skull

Correct: NKJV
Conservatives: 1
Liberals: 0
Corrupted: RV, ASV, RSV, NASV77, NIV, NASV95, NRSV, HCSB, NLT, ESV, MEV
Conservatives: 6
Liberals: 5
Conclusion: Except for the NKJV the conservatives are no better than the liberals. Anyone who agrees with this change or defends it should be consistent and scratch it out of every hymn in their hymn book and replace it with "skull." They

should also make it practice to **never again** use this "old," "archaic" 400 year old word when they are speaking!

Acts 3:13, 26; 4:27, 30

Problem: What we are studying here involves five verses. In the first four sets of verses are: **Acts 3:13, 3:26, 4:27** and **4:30**. In the two references in Acts 3 we find Jesus called the "Son" of God. In the two references in Acts 4 He is called God's holy "child." In modern versions all four of these references are changed to "servant" by faulty translation, thus eliminating four references to the sonship of Jesus Christ. The translators, whether conservative or liberal, justify this attack on Jesus Christ by claiming that the Greek word that the King James translators translated "Son" and "child" is actually the word for "servant." But, the fifth verse set puts the lie to this lame excuse because **all** of the versions that change "son/child" to "servant" translate the same Greek word as "son" in **John 4:51**! This kind of treatment of both Jesus Christ and "the original Greek" highlight the hypocrisy and dishonesty that is rampant among the translators of modern versions.

Example #1

Acts 3:13 KJB - The God of Abraham, and of Isaac, and of Jacob, the God of our fathers, hath glorified his **Son** Jesus; whom ye delivered up, and denied him in the presence of Pilate, when he was determined to let him go.

RV - Servant
ASV - Servant
RSV - servant
NASV77 - servant
NASV95 - servant
NRSV - servant
NLT - servant
HCSB - Servant

NIV - servant
NKJV - Servant
ESV - servant
MEV - Son

Correct: MEV
Conservatives: 1
Liberals: 0
Corrupted: RV, ASV, RSV, NASV77, NIV, NKJV, NASV95, NRSV, NLT, HCSB, ESV,
Conservatives: 6
Liberals: 5
Conclusion: Only one "conservative" translation got the verse right. The others join ranks with the liberals.

Example #2
Acts 3:26 KJB - Unto you first God, having raised up his **Son** Jesus, sent him to bless you, in turning away every one of you from his iniquities.

RV - Servant
ASV - Servant
RSV - servant
NASV77 - Servant
NIV - servant
NKJV - Servant
NASV95 - Servant
NRSV - servant
NLT - servant
HCSB - Servant
ESV - servant
MEV - Son

Correct: MEV
Conservatives: 1
Liberals: 0
Corrupted: RV, ASV, RSV, NASV77, NIV, NKJV, NASV95, NRSV, NLT, HCSB, ESV,
Conservatives: 6
Liberals: 5

Conclusion: Only one "conservative" translation got the verse right.

Example #3

Acts 4:27 KJB - For of a truth against thy holy **child** Jesus, whom thou hast anointed, both Herod, and Pontius Pilate, with the Gentiles, and the people of Israel, were gathered together,

RV - Servant
ASV - Servant
RSV - servant
NASV77 - servant
NIV - servant
NKJV - Servant
NASV95 - servant
NRSV - servant
NLT - servant
HCSB - Servant
ESV - servant
MEV - Son

Correct: MEV
Conservatives: 1
Liberals: 0
Corrupted: RV, ASV, RSV, NASV77, NIV, NKJV, NASV95, NRSV, NLT, HCSB, ESV,
Conservatives: 6
Liberals: 5
Conclusion: Again only the MEV got the verse right.

Example #4

Acts 4:30 KJB - By stretching forth thine hand to heal; and that signs and wonders may be done by the name of thy holy **child** Jesus.

RV - Servant
ASV - Servant
RSV - servant
NASV77 - servant
NASV95 - servant
NRSV - servant
NLT - servant
HCSB - Servant

NIV - servant
NKJV - Servant
ESV - servant
MEV - Son

Correct: MEV
Conservatives: 1
Liberals: 0
Corrupted: RV, ASV, RSV, NASV77, NIV, NKJV, NASV95, NRSV, NLT, HCSB, ESV,
Conservatives: 6
Liberals: 5
Conclusion: Once again only one "conservative" translation got the verse right.

Example #5
John 4:51 KJB - And as he was now going down, his servants met him, and told him, saying, Thy **son** liveth.

RV - son
ASV - son
RSV - son
NASV77 - son
NIV - boy
NKJV - son
NASV95 - son
NRSV - child
NLT - son
HCSB - boy
ESV - son
MEV - son

Correct: RV, ASV, RSV, NASV77, NIV, NKJV, NASV95, NRSV, NLT, HCSB, ESV, MEV
Conservatives: 7
Liberals: 5
Corrupted: None
Conservatives: 0
Liberals: 0

Conclusion: The conservatives are basically as bad as the liberals in these verses. By correctly translating the Greek word in John 4:51 **every modern translation** reveals that they **could have** allowed "Son" and "child" to remain in the first four references but instead stripped the Lord Jesus Christ of His sonship **four times**. What? Did you say you can find His sonship in other places in these modern translations? Fine, I can find it in the King James Bible in every reference you go to...**plus four more** that your weak, error-riddled modern translation doesn't have!

Acts 12:4

Problem: The meticulous student of scripture recognizes that if Peter was arrested during the Days of Unleavened Bread as it states in verse 3, then the Passover was already in the past. Thus, if Herod was going to wait until after the Passover he'd have to wait another year. But the pagan festival of Easter was just days away, thus he was waiting for **that day** to bring Peter out to the people. **Every single modern** translation, conservative or liberal mistranslates the Greek word "pascha" in this verse. Yes, "pascha" is the Greek word for "passover" but go ask a Greek, who speaks Greek, who lives in Greece what word he uses when he says, "Easter is coming."

KJB - And when he had apprehended him, he put him in prison, and delivered him to four quaternions of soldiers to keep him; intending after **Easter** to bring him forth to the people.

RV - the Passover
ASV - the Passover
RSV - the Passover
NASV77 - the Passover
NIV - the Passover
NASV95 - the Passover
NRSV - the Passover
NLT - the Passover
HCSB - the Passover
ESV - the Passover

NKJV - the Passover **MEV** - the Passover

Correct: None
Conservatives: 0
Liberals: 0
Corrupted: RV, ASV, RSV, NASV77, NIV, NKJV, NASV95, NRSV, NLT, HCSB, ESV, MEV
Conservatives: 7
Liberals: 5
Conclusion: None of the modern versions, whether they are conservative or liberal, has the correct translation in this case. There is no benefit to buying a "conservative" translation rather than a liberal one since both corrupt the text equally.

Galatians 5:12
Problem: There is quite a problem here and seems to be **more** than just translational. There are times throughout the Bible that God tells Israel to put someone out of their congregation for disciplinary reasons. When this form of punishment was exercised on anyone it says they were "cut off" from the congregation. (Ex. 12:15, 19; 30:38; 31:14; Lev. 7:20-27; 17:9, 14; 20:6; 22:3 just to denote a **few.**)

In Galatians the Apostle Paul is repairing the damage done to the church there when someone came into their congregation and convinced them that they needed to be circumcised and keep the law to be saved. In Gal. 5:13 he says he wishes these people were "cut off" from the congregation. Yet the twisted way in which this verse is defiled by **all** modern translators is a window through which we can view their perverted thinking process. It is degenerate and perverted.

QUESTION #76

KJB - I would they were even cut off which trouble you.
RV - I would that they which unsettle you would even **cut themselves off.**
ASV - I would that they that unsettle you would even **go beyond circumcision.**
RSV - I wish those who unsettle you would **mutilate themselves!**
NASV77 - Would that those who are troubling you would even **mutilate themselves.**
NIV - As for those agitators, I wish they would go the whole way and **emasculate themselves!**
NKJV - I could wish that those who trouble you would even **cut themselves off!**
NASV95 - I wish that those who are troubling you would even **mutilate themselves.**
NRSV - I wish those who unsettle you would **castrate themselves!**
NLT - I just wish that those troublemakers who want to mutilate you by circumcision would **mutilate themselves.**
HCSB - I wish those who are disturbing you might also **get themselves castrated!**
ESV - I wish those who unsettle you would **emasculate themselves!**
MEV - I wish that those who are troubling you would **castrate themselves!**

Correct: None
Conservatives: 0
Liberals: 0
Corrupted: RV, ASV, RSV, NASV77, NIV, NKJV, NASV95, NRSV, NLT, HCSB, ESV, MEV
Conservatives: 7

Liberals: 5
Conclusion: Being a "conservative" scholar apparently doesn't give one a mind any purer than that of a liberal.

I once saw a book entitled: *Unholy Hands on a Holy Book.* Every time I look at the perverted way that modern translators render this simple verse the title of that book comes to mind. What goes through their minds that whenever they see the words "cut off" the above perversions come to mind? Did **you** think the same as they when you read it?

Colossians 1:14
Problem: The Bible clearly states that ... without shedding of blood is no remission. (Heb.:22) We who have accepted Jesus Christ as our personal Saviour sing that we have been "washed in the blood." Yet the very payment that was made for our souls by Jesus Christ on the Cross comes under attack in many modern versions. In Col. 1:14 the words "through his blood" are removed in corrupt translations, whether or not they were translated by liberals or conservatives.
KJB - In whom we have redemption **through his blood**, even the forgiveness of sins:
RV - (Truth deleted)
ASV - (Truth deleted)
RSV - (Truth deleted)
NASV77 - (Truth deleted)
NIV - (Truth deleted)
NKJV - through His blood
NASV95 - (Truth deleted)
NRSV - (Truth deleted)
NLT - (Truth deleted)
HCSB - (Truth deleted)
ESV - (Truth deleted)
MEV - through His blood

Correct: NKJV, MEV
Conservatives: 2
Liberals: 0

QUESTION #76

Corrupted: RV, ASV, RSV, NASV77, NIV, NASV95, NRSV, NLT, HCSB, ESV
Conservatives: 5
Liberals: 5
Conclusion: Five of the conservative translations agree with the whole host of liberal translations that we do not gain our redemption "through his blood" while only two conservative translations hold the line of correct doctrine although both falter in other places.

2 Timothy 3:3
Problem: In prophesying about the last days, the Apostle Paul describes the many faults of the generation that will be alive at that time. In verse three he says they will be Without natural affection. What is it to be "without natural affection"? Homosexuality is "without natural affection." People who think that animals have rights are "without natural affection." those who would mourn a tree being cut down are "without natural affection."

In this verse the Holy Spirit arms the preacher of righteousness with the Scripture needed to exhort and rebuke those in these last days who are "without natural affection." But it appears that some who don't like their sins denounced think that all they have to do is alter the words that flowed from the mouth of God to eliminate the condemnation! Not only do they remove the scriptural denunciation of these perverts but they actually remove the weapon from the hand of the Man of God and place it in the hands of the very ones that the Scripture condemns. How many times have those who hold to the scriptural views of sexual perversion been called "unloving" by the very perverts described by the

Apostle? Well, thanks to the raft of modern versions they even have "scripture" to level at God's Bible believers.

Oh, and before you even go there, there is **no Greek authority** for **any** of these changes. The word translated "without natural affection" in this verse (and Romans 1:31) has only **one rendering allowed**, "no natural affection." anything else is a pervert trying to cover his tracks!

KJB - **Without natural affection**, trucebreakers, false accusers, incontinent, fierce, despisers of those that are good,

RV - without natural affection,
ASV - without natural affection,
RSV - inhuman,
NASV77 - unloving,
NIV - without love,
NKJV - unloving,
NASV95 - unloving,
NRSV - inhuman,
NLT - unloving,
HCSB - unloving,
ESV - heartless,
MEV - without natural affection,

Correct: RV, ASV, MEV
Conservatives: 2
Liberals: 1
Corrupted: RSV, NIV, NASV77, NKJV, NASV95, NRSV, ESV, NLT, HCSB,
Conservatives: 2
Liberals: 1
Conclusion: One liberal translation got it right while two conservative translations also did. The rest, "conservative" and liberal, faithfully corrupted the verse with absolutely **no Greek authority** for the changes they made. They simply **didn't like the plain truth** of the Bible and altered it according to their perverted values.

As you can see both the RV (1885) and ASV (1901) got the translation right. But that isn't because their translators were trying to be true to the text. It is because they were both the first of their kind and were being cautious with their changes. In succeeding revisions of both versions they later corrupted the verse with a translation that is unsupported by the Greek. Even the so-called NKJV abandoned the truth.

1 John 5:7

Problem: This is the greatest **single verse** confirming the existence of the Triune God. Yet this great truth is not necessarily sacred to those translators that call themselves "conservative" for they attack the verse with all the venom of a Jehovah's Witness!

In most cases when a modern translation removes a verse from the text they do not alter the verse numbering. Therefore, when they remove Matt. 17:21 from the text we find that following verse 20 is verse 22! Similarly, when they remove Matt. 18:11 from the text we find that verse 10 is followed by verse 12 with a curious gap in the numbering cycle.

But in this case they are trying to destroy the greatest verse on the Trinity. (If you reject that word then refer to the Triune God as the "Godhead" if your prefer.) Here they shamelessly attempt to deceive their readers by extracting verse seven and then splitting either verse six or verse eight to create a **false** verse seven. If they split verse 6 they take the last phrase of the verse, And it is the Spirit that beareth witness, because the Spirit is truth. and place it in the blank spot left by their theft. If they split verse 7 they snatch the first few words of verse 8, **splitting a sentence**, and place "And there are three that bare witness..." in the space where verse 7 belongs. If this were done in a legal document these people would go to jail.

But since it is "only" the **perfect words of God** they are defacing they go to the bank instead!

KJB - For there are three that bear record in heaven, the Father, the Word, and the Holy Ghost: and these three are one.

RV - And it is the Spirit that beareth witness, because the Spirit is the truth. (Splits verse 6)

ASV - And it is the Spirit that beareth witness, because the Spirit is the truth. (Splits verse 6)

RSV - And the Spirit is the witness, because the Spirit is the truth. (Splits verse 6)

NASV77 - And the Spirit is the witness, because the Spirit is the truth. (Splits verse 6)

NIV - For there are three that testify: (Splits verse 8)

NKJV - For there are three that bear witness in heaven: the Father, the Word, and the Holy Spirit; and these three are one.

NASV95 - For there are three that testify: (Splits verse 8)

NRSV - There are three that testify: (Splits verse 8)

NLT - So we have these three witnesses- (Splits verse 8)

HCSB - For there are three that testify: (Splits verse 8)

ESV - For there are three that testify: (Splits verse 8)

MEV - There are three who testify in heaven: the Father, the Word, and the Holy Spirit, and the three are one.

Correct: NKJV, MEV
Conservatives: 2
Liberals: 0
Corrupt:
Split verse 6 - RV, ASV, RSV & the NASV77
Conservatives: 2
Liberals: 2

Split verse 8 - NIV, NASV95, NRSV, NLT, HCSB & the ESV

Conservatives: 3

Liberals: 3

Conclusion: Only the NKJV and the MEV leave the verse unmolested while five of the so-called "conservative" translations agree with all of the liberal translations that it is a mistake to have the verse in the Bible. So five of the conservative translations are not a source to be trusted for sound doctrine. (Notice that both the RV of 1885, and the ASV of 1901 originally split verse 6 but later editions split verse 8.)

Here we find that two of the conservative translations agree with two of the liberal translations and corrupt the verse while three of the liberals join with the conservatives and have the reading correct. Here, trusting a "conservative" translation isn't a safe course because it doesn't guarantee that it will not corrupt the Scripture.

Conclusion

An objective study of both groups of translations reveals that the problem has nothing to do with conservative or liberal theology. **The problem is scholarship itself, whether it is conservative or liberal.** Neither you nor I have the right to defend even one assault on the word and words of God whether they are made by someone with whom we agree or not. If you know someone who adheres to any of the corruptions you have just seen I don't say that they hate God or even that they are unsaved. But, **they are not** true to the words of God and their opinions and declarations concerning modern translations are not to be given any weight whatsoever.

You may use a modern translation and excuse your infidclity to the words of God by claiming these are just a few little changes. First, they are not little! As to being "few," if you were on a boat and it were to have as many holes in its bottom as there are corruptions in the Bible, how many holes are you willing to accept in your boat?

Question #77

Question: For study purposes isn't it better to use several versions rather than restricting yourself to just one?

Answer: Absolutely not!

Explanation: Sadly, the obvious answer to this question reveals the **good sense** some unsaved people have as compared to deceived and stupid Christians.

Some years ago a Christian young man was engaged in a conversation with fourteen unsaved young men. The general response to this young man by this group of non-believers was, "If God **really** wrote the Bible there would only be **one Bible** and not so many."

Many Christians who have attempted to witness to Muslims have been rebuffed by the simple argument, "The Bible cannot be God's word because there would only be one, but there are many. That is why the Koran is God's word, because there is only one."

Many innocent Christians are led astray by another Christian, maybe even a preacher, who advises them to abandon any absolute authority and simply pick four or five modern versions to use. (During our 1995 appearance on the John Ancherberg television show James White did this very thing. When asked by the Host to recommend a modern version White said he didn't recommend one version but said Christians should consult three or four of their choice.)

This naive approach overlooks one insurmountable problem. Of the scores of modern versions the Christian has to pick from, which ones should he consider and which should he not consider? You see, **everybody** rejects some kind of a modern version.

This problem is similar to the one loose Christians have when talking about dress standards. They will tell a "legalist" friend, "I don't believe we should mandate what people can and cannot wear." But that isn't actually true. For, although he may not care if a woman wears pants or a dress to church, I can guarantee that if a woman comes to his church wearing a halter top and a very revealing miniskirt he will suddenly think that we **should** tell **some** people how to dress. Why? Because **everybody** has standards of some kind!

Those who might recommend that a Christian just choose several modern versions may, upon being shown which ones they acquired say, "Oh! Well, you should use **that one.**" Why? Because **everybody** rejects one version or another for one reason or another.

So you see, **every Christian** believes in a Final Authority. Bible believers make that authority the Bible, and when they say that they mean the **King James** Bible. Christians who want to escape the dictatorial power of the Bible will claim that any version will do. But, **there is always** a modern version they will advise against, thus moving the power of Final Authority from the **Bible** and placing it on themselves.

A great man once said, "The bottom line on this subject is: Either the **Bible** is **in subjection to you,** or **you are in subjection to the Bible.**"

In which position are you?

Question #78

Question: How important is having a "perfect" Bible anyway?

Answer: It's the most important item you can possess.

Explanation: If it were not for the Bible we would all be lost in spiritual darkness and on our way to Hell. Some proclaim that salvation comes through the death, burial and resurrection of Jesus Christ, not by possessing a Bible. Correct. But how would we **know** about the death, burial and resurrection of Jesus Christ if the Bible didn't exist to tell us? And if the Bible is incorrect in one area or another then how do we know it's correct concerning what it teaches about our salvation?

If you need food you go to a grocery store. Most people have several different grocery store chains in their city. If they don't like one, they can always go to another.

If you wish to continue your education after high school, you can go to college. Which one? Any one you choose. There are innumerable choices to pick from.

If you need a new car and don't like Fords you can buy a Chevrolet...or any number of the brands offered on the open market.

But the Bible is the **only source** of spiritual truth. There is no other option. If the Bible can be eliminated or neutered, then we are blind to spiritual truth and the lost are damned.

Sometimes you can use pliers instead of a wrench, a pocket knife instead of a screw driver. But if there is no Bible there is **nothing** to replace it. The Bible fulfills innumerable needs in the life of men, **even** unsaved men. The Bible is:

1. Our Communication from God - God doesn't come "glowing" in our bedrooms to deliver us His messages. He doesn't stand 90 feet tall in our backyards and threaten to kill us if we fail to raise enough money. And He **is not** those voices in your head! God communicates to us through His words as found in the Bible.

If that Bible can be corrupted or rendered questionable, our communication from Him is void and **there is no other option**.

2. How we find out how to be saved - You may be able to win someone to the Lord without a physical Bible present but not without quoting it. You cannot describe Christ's virgin birth, deity, death, burial & resurrection without learning about them through the Bible. Neither can you reveal that Eternal Life is just a prayer away without referring to the Bible.

Everything we **know** about creation, Christ and salvation could be just as true as they are but without the Bible we would be ignorant of them.

3. Where we get our doctrine from - The Bible is far more than just a really big Gospel tract to be used to lead lost souls to Christ. It is **the only textbook** that tells us how the world got here, why we are here and what we can do to make our lives truly meaningful. Anything else is just some feeble-brained man's opinion, his philosophy of life, or, as the fuzzy-brained designer-coffee crowd would say it, "my truth." In other words it's more useless than a politician's promise.

4. Our weapon against the devil - Somebody hates you. No, I'm not referring to anyone in your family, at your place of work or in some evil foreign country. Lost or saved, the devil hates all of Mankind. He is an "Equal Opportunity Hater." His passive attention via corrupt world systems has damned billions of people over the centuries. But his personal attention can buckle the knees, break the will or destroy the life of God's very best. As horrifying and ghastly as physical combat is, the devil's spiritual combat yields a greater prize than land, freedom or even life. It deals in souls.

Many Christians have experienced satanic spiritual attacks in their lives. Many times a Christian will say they had to "Plead the Blood" during one of these episodes. Yet "pleading the Blood" is not what protects one from the power of the Satan. Yes, we who are saved have overcome Satan's desire to damn our souls by the Blood of the Lamb of God, the Lord Jesus Christ. But "the Blood" is not the shield or weapon prescribed to resist or attack the devil. It is God's word, the Bible.

The devil possesses far more power than **any** human being. Nothing we do on our own can resist him or overcome him. Therefore God has supplied us with an eternal, undefeatable weapon for our combat, the Bible.

In describing the power of the devil in Job, chapter 40, God reveals a great and reassuring truth in verse 19. He is the chief of the ways of God: he that made him can make his sword to approach unto him. The Bible informs us that ...the sword...is the word of God. (Eph 6:17)

After 40 days of fasting, Jesus Christ "climbed into the ring" with the greatest power of evil in the universe, the devil...**and knocked him right out through the ropes with**

three punches, "it is written", "it is written","it is written"! Not "plead the Blood", "plead the Blood", "plead the Blood."

You should learn and memorize Scripture for those trials when Satan is close at hand and leaning heavily on you. Don't "plead the Blood." **Quote the Book!**

The Bible is the sole source of all that we know about God, Heaven & our future. You need it far more than the latest Christian music album or your apostate church's laser light show!

Question #79

Question: Scholars are constantly looking for more manuscripts of the New Testament. Don't we just need to find a few more manuscripts to settle the issue of which Bible is the perfect word of God?

Answer: No.

Explanation: This statement sounds reasonable but there are several realities that prove its insincerity.

There are many ancient writings to which man, rightfully or not, ascribes great value. Also though the opinions and teachings of philosophers and playwrights are overrated and many times incorrect, mankind puts great value on them. This is done mainly to offer rebellious Man an alternative to the divine decrees of God. Of the outstanding historical writers there not a great many manuscript witnesses available. The general consensus is:

1. **Socrates,** 470 - 399 BC: There are only 7 copies of his writings in existence.
2. **Plato,** 428/427 or 424/423 - 348/347 BC : There are about 250 copies of Plato's writing extant.
3. **Aristotle,** 384 - 322 BC: He wrote over 200 treatise but only 31 survive.
4. **Aristophanes,** 900 AD: Only 10 copies of his writing exist.

5. Shakespeare, April 1564 - April 23, 1616 AD: Shakespeare wrote at least 38 plays and over 150 short and long poems.

There are 5,889 manuscript witnesses to the text of the New Testament. Many errantly repeat a figure of around 5,500 witnesses. But this figure generally originates from Kurt Alands list of extant manuscripts published back in 1994. Since that time there have been numerous discoveries of more New Testament witnesses. In a work separate from this one this author has published the most up-to-date catalog on New Testament Greek witnesses which comes to the figure given above.

If the above paltry number of witnesses for secular historical writers suffices for the authority of the texts of their writings then **no honest person** can claim a need to uncover even one more manuscript witness for the Bible, either Old or New Testament.

Secondly, the pious sounding claim that scholars are meticulously looking everywhere for more manuscript witnesses of the Bible is grossly misleading. They aren't. Actually scholars are meticulously looking everywhere for more manuscript witnesses of the Alexandrian Text of the New Testament in hopes of overthrowing the merit of the King James Bible.

This is neither a falsehood nor an overstatement. In the case of both the Old and New Testaments, scholars **leap** at any new manuscript discovery hoping to find a witness that will further this agenda. Once a manuscript is examined and found to undergird the text of the King James Bible, it is flippantly dismissed and pushed to obscurity.

QUESTION #79

The Dead Sea Scrolls illustrate this prejudice concerning the Old Testament. When the Dead Sea Scrolls were discovered in Qumran in 1948, scholars hoped they would support the Old Testament text that was being presented as superior to that used for the King James Bible. Once translation of the scrolls began it became apparent they were not witnesses **against** the traditional Old Testament but actually reenforced its superiority. Therefore they were dismissed as irrelevant and locked away from public examination.

This very same animosity for the KJB has driven the search for New Testament witnesses. **Countless times** scholars have excitedly rushed to a new manuscript discovery hoping for an ally in their battle against the traditional New Testament text only to be demoralized by the **reality** that the newly found witness **did indeed** testify to the original text of the New Testament just as it is accurately reproduced in the King James Bible.

This excitement is similar to that of NASA scientists desperate to prove evolution. They send out countless landers to moons and planets. Prior to these landings they triumphantly proclaim that their space equipment is about to discover evidence that confirms evolution. Then, after digging, probing and analyzing the samples obtained by their mechanical savior and finding it does nothing of the kind they casually dismiss their lack of evidence by claiming they landed in the wrong spot or some other scientific fairy tale.

Scholars subject every newly discovered manuscript to a series of Test case scripture references in order to identify it as Antiochan or Alexandrian. Upon discovery that it is **one more** of the massive body of witnesses to the original New

Testament as faithfully reproduced in the King James Bible the very same scholars that lauded it as a hopeful ally casually dismiss it as another false witness of the text they hate.

This very thing happened in 2008 when eight formerly unknown manuscripts of the New Testament were discovered in Albania. Like desperate NASA scientists, "Bible scholars" rushed to examine them in vain hope that they would affirm their errant position. One-by-one as the manuscripts were checked against their Test case list of scripture it was discovered that, one by one, they testified on behalf of the hated King James text. Suddenly their importance was discounted and they were reluctantly added to the New Testament manuscript catalog of witnesses while the discouraged scholars ran off looking for any other new discoveries that could be used to reenforce their errant position.

Please understand, these **same scholars** will boldly include these manuscripts in the overall **general** number of witnesses for the New Testament when comparing God's divine Book to the writing of uninspired historical writers.

Case-in-point: In northern Kentucky, not far from the Cincinnati International Airport is a novel public attraction entitled The Ark Encounter. (It was constructed in conjunction with The Creation Science Museum 45 minutes away. I urge **anyone** to visit both attractions. Set aside at least one day for each. They are worth the price of admission. You will be greatly impressed with both the quality and accuracy of these biblical presentations.)

The Ark Encounter is a life-size representation of what the creators believe to be an accurate reproduction the both the size and design of Noah's Ark. Their arguments are well presented and merit careful consideration, not off-handed dismissal.

Visitors to the Ark Encounter enter the Ark in the first deck level and are educated as to construction, animal care and then human housing on Noah's Ark as they slowly progress to the top, third level. On this third level are also found spiritual video presentations including an excellent presentation of the Gospel.

Also among these video presentations is an excellent video that compares the number of manuscript witnesses for secular writers as opposed to the witnesses for the New Testament. The man in this video uses coffee beans for this presentation: One bean equating to one manuscript witness. He lays on the table before him the few beans that represent some of the writers mentioned above. When he's finished with the secular writers he stands there with everything from a few scattered beans to a tiny mound of coffee beans.

Then, from the floor he retrieves **a entire bag** of coffee beans and dumps them on the table, creating a **mountain** of coffee beans and impressively, and **correctly** declares these to be the overwhelming number of witnesses to the Bible. It is well done and impressive.

Unfortunately, most visitors have no idea of one, **massive fact** that **is not** revealed in this video. After the man has dumped the bag of beans on the table, he could then have grabbed a handful of those beans, hardly diminishing the size of the mountain, and placed them beside this mountain of coffee beans and say, "Now this little handful of beans represents the text of the bible versions used in the Ark Encounter."

You see, as the visitor slowly progresses from Level One to Level Three they will read facts and figures about the ark and then read strange renditions of scripture that **are not** from the King James Bible but from modern versions based on **a handful of flawed manuscripts** originating in Alexandria, Egypt, that have been interpreted according to the corrupt Alexandrian Mentality. Although the creators of the Ark Encounter have well-founded faith in the accuracy of the Bible's historic account of Noah's Ark, they sadly lack the faith to believe God has a perfect Book **on this planet**. The "perfect Bible" they talk about actually only exists in their philosophical minds for, if asked to put a copy of that "perfect Bible" they trumpet in a Believer's hand, **if honest**, they would have to confess that they don't believe there is a perfect, flawless copy existing anywhere on the planet.

This is no idle charge nor vicious attack. They have done a fabulous job of representing the true historic account of Noah's Ark. But they don't believe the Bible they got this account from is **word perfect**.

Why? Because, just as **I** concede to the representation of something I completely believe in, Noah's Ark, but have not personally researched to reproduce an accurate copy as they have, I **defer** to their expertise in the subject. They, on the other hand, have **deferred** to the tainted opinion of "Christian Scholarship" on a subject they have not personally researched in an effort to reproduce an accurate copy of the Bible.

So, the irrefutable fact is that we don't require even **one more** manuscript witness to establish the reliability of the Bible, the King James Bible. The other irrefutable fact is that if a new manuscript witness of the Bible is discovered it will just be **one more witness for the King James Bible** and therefore will quickly be dismissed as unimportant and ignored by scholars whose prejudice preempts their honesty.

Question #80

Question: Aren't we moving nearer to having a perfect Bible with each new version?

Answer: No.

Explanation: Modern versions exhibit Progressive Degradation with each edition of the same version.

Bible publishing houses love to trumpet their latest money-making hope as being easier to read and closer to the Originals. This is, of course, insincere nonsense. They couldn't care less about their newest version being easy to read, free of archaic words or closer to the original autographs. **They care about making money!**

The other half of the bible making industry are those select few professional textual critics who do the translation work. They portray themselves as earnest purveyors of biblical truth who are ever "fine tuning" their works to eliminate the remaining flaws, producing as close to a perfect and reliable translation as possible. This is also baloney. This is a closed group that sits on the well-cap of biblical manuscripts and fears losing control of the flow of information. **None of them** believe there ever was or ever can be a perfect Bible and hate those fanatics (**us!**) who actually believe the Bible is perfect.

But I said that modern versions suffer from Progressive Degradation and wish to show that that is not just a simple derogatory statement about new versions but is an actual phenomenon that occurs with the continual regurgitation of the corruption flowing from the fount of Alexandria.

Example #1 - The Degressive Editions of the Revised Version

While the Revised Version (RV) of 1884 was not the first translation of the long-rejected Alexandrian Text, it was the first initiated by an ecclesiastical body, the Anglican Church, of England. It had little impact and was redone and issued in 1954 as the Revised Standard Version (RSV). This lame translation was so repulsive that it was mocked as the "Communist Version" and rejected by the public at large. (It should be noted that the majority of sales for these corruptions of scripture occur because a money-laden denomination decried them as their "official" translation and buys thousands of them. Then, as time goes on the translation drifts into oblivion and is allowed to die. Then the denomination repeats the process with a new version.) The RSV died of well-placed neglect and was resuscitated in 1999 and reissued as the New Revised Standard Version (NRSV).

We will examine these three versions and see if the revised version got better or worse with each new iteration. The words in question will be in bold type for easy identification.

1. Psalm 12:6, 7

RV - 6 The words of the LORD are pure words; As silver tried in a furnace on the earth, Purified seven times.

7 **Thou shalt keep them,** O LORD, Thou shalt preserve them from this generation for ever.

RSV - 6 The promises of the Lord are promises that are pure, silver refined in a furnace on the ground, purified seven times.

7 Do thou, O Lord, **protect us, guard us** ever from this generation.

NRSV - 6 The promises of the Lord are promises that are pure, silver refined in a furnace on the ground, purified seven times.

7 You, O Lord, will **protect us; you will guard us** from this generation forever.

Psalm 12:6 & 7 are the **bedrock verses** that every Bible believer runs to to prove that God not only inspired His words but promised to **preserve** them. As you can see that divine promise was maintained in the RV but was eliminated in the later RSV and NRSV which both alter God's divine preservation to the poor of verse 5 rather than the "words" of verse 6.

There is only one reason for doing this. Modern translators not only do not believe in the divine preservation of scripture but they realize that if God's people read Psalm 12:6, 7 that they will ask the simple question, "Then where is God's preserved Bible?" A short study of the version God used throughout history will lead them straight to the King James Bible. They can't have that!

In order to eradicate God's promise they **make up** a translation that has **no foundation in any Hebrew manuscript on earth!** For you see, the Hebrew of verse 7 **in every extant manuscript containing Psalm 12**, is **third person plural** (they, them) not **first person plural**, (we, us). Thus, by their actions the translators of the latter two revised versions **invented a Hebrew text** just for the purpose of destroying God's true words.

2. John 3:16

RV - For God so loved the world, that he gave his **only begotten Son,** that whosoever believeth on him should not perish, but have eternal life.

RSV - For God so loved the world that he gave his **only Son,** that whoever believes in him should not perish but have eternal life.

NRSV - For God so loved the world that he gave his **only Son,** so that everyone who believes in him may not perish but may have eternal life.

Here we see that, even though the RV was lacking in many other places it correctly translated the Greek word, "monogenes:" "mono" - one, only; "genes" - generated, begotten. By failing to translate the plain Greek the revisers have **inserted a contradiction** into the canon of scripture.

In Romans 8:14, 19 believers are referred to as the "sons of God." (John 1:12) We who have accepted Jesus Christ as our Saviour are God's **spiritual** sons, but **not** His **begotten** sons. We have been born to Him in the spirit but not begotten in the flesh as Jesus Christ was. Jesus was God's only **begotten** Son.

3. Romans 8:14, 19

RV - 14 For as many as are led by the Spirit of God, these are **sons of God.**

19 For the earnest expectation of the creation waiteth for the revealing of the **sons of God.**

RSV - 14 For all who are led by the Spirit of God are **sons of God.**

19 For the creation waits with eager longing for the revealing of the **sons of God;**

NRSV - 14 For all who are led by the Spirit of God are **children of God.**

19 For the creation waits with eager longing for the revealing of the **children of God;**

Here we see that both the RV and RSV contain "sons of God." In the case of the RV this is no problem since it correctly translated John 3:16. But the text of the RSV now contains the above mentioned contradiction. The NRSV seeks to duck the issue and crow "We're gender neutral" and inserts "children of God;". But God has only two kinds of children male (sons), or female (daughters). (The 52 other genders imagined by perverted liberals are as illegitimate as homosexual marriage.)

4. John 18:36

RV - Jesus answered, My kingdom is not of this world: if my kingdom were of this world, then would my servants fight, that I should not be delivered to the Jews: but **now** is my kingdom not from hence.

RSV - Jesus answered, "My kingship is not of this world; if my kingship were of this world, my servants would fight, that I might not be handed over to the Jews; but my kingship is not from the world."

NRSV - Jesus answered, "My kingdom is not from this world. If my kingdom were from this world, my followers would be fighting to keep me from being handed over to the Jews. But as it is, my kingdom is not from here."

When responding to Pilate's question of whether or not He was the King of the Jews, Jesus Christ made it plain that He did indeed have a kingdom but it simply wasn't here "now." The Greek word for "now", "nun," is in **every** extant copy of John 18:36 and the translators of the RV were correct to bravely translate it. But, as the RV continued its journey through time it also continued its journey through corruption with both the RSV and the NRSV refusing to grant Jesus Christ a kingdom on this earth even if the Greek text did!

Thus we see that the "revised versions" drifted farther from biblical and translational accuracy with each update, obvious evidence of Progressive Degradation.

Example #2 - The Degressive Editions of the Living Bible
1. 1 Samuel 13:1
KJB - Saul reigned **one year;** and when he had reigned **two years** over Israel,
LB, 1971 - one year...two years...
NLT, 2015 - Saul was **thirty years old** when he became king, and he reigned for **forty-two years**.

2. Luke 16:23
KJB - **And in hell** he lift up his eyes, being in torments, and seeth Abraham afar off, and Lazarus in his bosom.
LB, 1971 - in hell
NLT, 2015 - and he went to the place of the dead.

3. Acts 26:14
KJB - And when we were all fallen to the earth, I heard a voice speaking unto me, and saying in the **Hebrew** tongue, Saul, Saul, why persecutest thou me? it is hard for thee to kick against the pricks.
LB, 1971 - Hebrew
NLT, 2015 -"Aramaic

Here we see that, as bad as the original Living Bible was it had 1 Samuel 13:1 correct. But, when it was revised the translators caved in to peer pressure and followed the other modern versions with a translation that **they all know** has no basis in the Hebrew.

Next we see they went weak-kneed over the word "hell" and gave us the lame translation, "...the place of the dead," whatever that is?

Finally these "blind" translators also followed their "blind leaders" and translated the Greek word, "Hebros" as "Aramaic" in order to grease the rails for the false teaching of the Roman Catholic Church that Jesus spoke Aramaic. Thus, again we see Progressive Degradation in action.

Example #3 - The Degressive Editions of the New International Version

Luke 16:23

KJB - And in hell he lift up his eyes, being in torments, and seeth Abraham afar off, and Lazarus in his bosom.

NIV, 1973 - in hell

NIV, 2011 - in hades

Once again we see Progressive Degradation take its toll on an already flawed translation as the revisers of the corrupt NIV made it even more so by eliminating all references to "hell" and went straight to "hades."

Example #4 - The Degressive Editions of the New King James Version

Zechariah 13:6

KJB - And one shall say unto him, What are these **wounds in thine hands?**

NKJV, 1982 - What are these **wounds in your hands?**

NKJV, 1994 - What are these **wounds between your arms**?

QUESTION #80

The 1994 revision of the NKJV was so secret that to this day many have no idea it took place. But there is no more glaring change than the removal of this reference to the crucifixion of Jesus Christ. In just barely more than a decade the NKJV turned from sound doctrine to false doctrine.

Example #5 - The Degressive Editions of the American Standard Version

1. 1 Samuel 13;1

KJB - Saul reigned **one year;** and when he had reigned **two years** over Israel,

ASV, 1901 - Saul was **forty years old** when he began to reign; and when he **had reigned two years** over Israel,

NASV, 1964 - Saul was **forty years old** when he began to reign, and he reigned **thirty-two years** over Israel.

NASV, 1977 - Saul was **forty years old** when he began to reign, and he reigned **thirty-two years** over Israel.

NASV, 1995 - Saul was **thirty years old** when he began to reign, and he reigned **forty two years** over Israel.

Here we see that the translators of the various American Standard Versions weren't stable enough to maintain a standard reading in its four editions. The ASV of 1901 corrupted the first half of the verse but left the latter half correct. Then the next two editions, 1964 and 1977, corrupted the remainder of the verse. Then the translators felt insecure when they saw how the verse was handled in other modern versions so they switched the two errant readings for 1995!

You may say that these aren't major problems. Fine. Then please contact the translators of the 1995 edition and ask them if the 1901, 1964 and 1977 editions **were wrong.**

2. John 1:18

KJB - No man hath seen God at any time; the only begotten **Son,** which is in the bosom of the Father, he hath declared him.

ASV, 1901 - No man hath seen God at any time; the only begotten **Son,** who is in the bosom of the Father, he hath declared him.

NASV, 1964 - No man has seen God at any time; the only begotten **God,** who is in the bosom of the Father, He has explained Him.

NASV, 1977 - No man has seen God at any time; the only begotten **God,** who is in the bosom of the Father, He has explained Him.

NASV, 1995 - No one has seen God at any time; the only begotten **God** who is in the bosom of the Father, He has explained Him.

As the reader can see, the ASV of 1901 correctly declared Jesus was God's only begotten **Son**. But by 1964 the translators believed He was a begotten "God," just like the Jehovah's Witnesses believe. The 1977 and 1995 editions never corrected this trip into Progressive Degradation.

3. John 18:36

KJB - Jesus answered, My kingdom is not of this world: if my kingdom were of this world, then would my servants fight, that I should not be delivered to the Jews: but **now** is my kingdom not from hence.

ASV, 1901 - Jesus answered, My kingdom is not of this world: if my kingdom were of this world, then would my servants fight, that I should not be delivered to the Jews: but **now** is my kingdom not from hence.

NASV, 1964 - Jesus answered, " My kingdom is not of this world. If My kingdom were of this world, then My servants would be

fighting, that I might not be delivered up to the Jews; but as it is, My kingdom is not of this realm." **NASV, 1977** - Jesus answered, " My kingdom is not of this world. If My kingdom were of this world, then My servants would be fighting, that I might not be delivered up to the Jews; but as it is, My kingdom is not of this realm."
NASV, 1995 - Jesus answered, "My kingdom is not of this world. If My kingdom were of this world, then My servants would be fighting so that I would not be handed over to the Jews; but as it is, My kingdom is not of this realm."

4. Galatians 5:12
KJB - I would they were even cut off which trouble you.
ASV, 1901 - I would that they that unsettle you would even **go beyond circumcision.**
NASV, 1964 - Would that those who are troubling you would even **mutilate themselves.**
NASV, 1977 - Would that those who are troubling you would even **mutilate themselves.**
NASV, 1995 - I wish that those who are troubling you would even **mutilate themselves.**

We Bible believers refer to modern versions as "perversions" and seldom does that description fit as well as it does as when studying the renderings of Galatians 5:12. Here we see the translators, whose minds must be constantly submerged in sexually perverted thoughts spew their depraved view of inspired Scripture.

While the "...go beyond circumcision." of the ASV of 1901 leaves some room for argument as to just what they wished to say the 1964 edition, and beyond, leave no doubt as to the perverted thoughts of their translators. If you agree with these three perverted renderings of the **divine** words of God you will have to convince yourself that this depraved interpretation is what the **Holy** Spirit of God had in mind when He inspired the Apostle Paul. Good luck!

Thus we see the Progressive Degradation is the standard course for modern translations. What does this mean? It means that if you are using a modern translation that does not pervert the words of God as you've seen above and elsewhere in this book you **can't be sure** future editions won't.

Question #81

Question: Why should we believe the KJB is the Word of God & not another English version?

Answer: The King James Bible is the only Bible that is not a "One Man" or "One Group" translation.

Explanation: (Be advised, anyone who tries to answer authoritatively the question, "Why the King James Bible?" is claiming to speak directly for God. Therefore, I never claim to know why God chose to use the KJB. What I do is observe some historic facts and then try to reach a reasonable explanation.)

To address the question, "Why the KJB and not another English version?" you must divide the question into two halves:

1. "Why the KJB and not a pre-King James English version?"
2. "Why the KJB and not a post-King James English version?"

1. Why not a pre-King James English translation?

As I've said, I cannot declare that the following are the reasons for God not using a pre-KJB translation. I can only examine the historic evidence.

A. The Translations: Every pre-KJB translation was either a "one man" or "one group" translation.

1. "One Man" Translations
The Wycliff Bible - 1380
The Tyndale Bible - 1525
The Coverdale Bible - 1535
The Mathews Bible - 1537
The Great Bible - 1538
The Richard Taverner Bible - 1539

2. "One Group" Translations
The Geneva (Puritan) -1560
The Bishops' (Anglican) - 1568[3]
The Douey-Rheims (Roman Catholic) - 1582

The King James was neither. It was translated by a committee made of both Anglicans & Puritans. That would be like saying it was translated by Democrats and Republicans. The Anglicans kept it from being a purely Puritan translation and the Puritans kept it from being a purely Anglican translation.

The truly mindless hater of the King James Bible who never thinks but tries to spin everything to hurt the Bible will attempt to use this "two party system" in a disparaging way, but we can't be concerned with enlightening the politicians, only the thinkers.

B. The English Language: Also concerning pre-KJB translations is the issue of the English language itself.

---

3. I've given the dates for the publication of the entire Bible; sometimes the New Testament was published years before the Old Testament, such as the Geneva: NT 1557, entire Bible, 1560.

1. English developed in three phases:
Old English: 449 AD - 1100 AD
Middle English: 1100 AD - 1450 AD
Modern English: 1450 AD - Present

Because the printing font used by the printers of the original King James Bible was Gothic many think it was printed in Old English. No. We couldn't read either Old or even Middle English. (More on this subject under another question.) They would appear as foreign languages to us. Although spelling was still in flux, the foundational structure of Modern English finished it's development at the end of the 16th Century (1500's). Thus, every pre-KJB translation was translated into a still developing, unstable language. In spite of the font used, and the less than honest claims of its detractors, the King James was the first translation done in Modern English.

2. Why the KJV and not a post-King James English version?

The case of the Post-KJB translation is a bit easier to define. Every translation since 1611 is based on both flawed Greek witnesses or fatally tainted scholarship.

A. The Witnesses: Prior to 1611 all English translations were products of the Textus Receptus which faithfully represents the text of the Originals and is vastly superior to the Critical Text used to translate modern versions. This Critical Text (its official name) is based on inferior Greek witnesses originating in Alexandria, Egypt. When pure text manuscripts arrived in Alexandria non-believers there edited them, removing verses that didn't agree with their unregenerate thinking. Thus, one of the hallmarks of modern translations is their weakening of biblical doctrines. (Deity of Christ, the Trinity, etc.)

B. Modern scholarship: The plethora of modern translations are also victims of fatally tainted scholarship such as; Westcott & Hort who publicly admitted to viewing the Bible as not inspired by God but just another book such as Shakespeare, or by men like Philip Schaff and Bruce Metzger who were students of unbelieving German rationalism and did all within their power to sabotage the true words of God.

In the case of the New King James Version, which makes the claim to a Majority Text base rather than a Critical Text base there are numerous problems. Since this is by no means an attempt at a thorough expose I'll illustrate the simple truth that it is harder to read than the King James Bible. Yes, in spite of the propaganda you've heard, the NKJV is harder to read than the KJB. Let the reader simply examine Titus 1:6 in a King James Bible and a NKJV with a little honesty and integrity and see what happens to the simple terms "riot" and "unruly" of the KJB and this will be obvious. There are several publications that go into the NKJV problems more thoroughly so I won't rewrite what has already been written.

Question #82

Question: The Geneva Bible came before the King James. Why isn't it the perfect word of God?

Answer: Because, good as it is, it has mistakes in it.

Explanation: Around 2007 a Bible was widely distributed to Bible believers as the 1599 Geneva Bible. Its promoters made the very claim that since it was translated from the Textus Receptus and was published prior to the King James Bible it was somehow superior to the KJB.

The first problem with this claim was that it **wasn't** a 1599 Geneva Bible. It stated clearly for all to see in the introduction that it was a reproduction of a 2006 **update** of the Geneva Bible. Defend it all you want but that is simply false advertising. Remember, the English language did not finish its development until around 1600. The Geneva was first published in 1557. The publishers knew that today's readers would never be able to read a true 1599 Geneva so they updated it and then claimed it was a 1599. Do you think that's a proper way to sell a Bible?

The producers of the 1599 (2006) Geneva Bible didn't even take a 1599 and update or clarify it. They started with a failed publication of an updated version that was published in 2003 by L. L. Brown. How do I know? Duh, I read it on the first page of the Preface where it plainly states, "Our source copy was published by L. L. Brown (the 1599 Geneva Bible, Ozark, MO: L. L. Brown Publishing, 7th printing, 2003)"

Why was this edition not a authentic 1599?

1. They had radically modernized the spelling. In the 2006 Geneva Bible John 3:16 reads as follows:

John 3:16, 2006 GB - For God so loveth the world, that he hath given his only begotten Son, that whosoever believeth in him, should not perish, but have everlasting life.

How does that verse appear in an authentic Geneva Bible?

John 3:16, 1599 GB - For God so loueth the world, that he hath geuen his only begotten Sonne, that whosoever beleueth in him, should not peryshe, but haue euerlasting lyfe.[4]

Now imagine reading an entire Bible printed like that.

The proponents of the 2006 Geneva Bible might respond that the "1611" King James Bible that we use today has **also** had its spelling updated over the years and that, in fact, we actually use a 1769 edition rather than a true 1611. True, but they don't have 1611 printed on the cover. Also, proponents of the King James Bible call it the "1611" because that was the year it was published. For example, the 1911 Colt Automatic Pistol has been around since that year, which was the year it was issued. Today you can purchase a Colt "1911" that has features it didn't have back in 1911. You can even buy one that is a different caliber than the original .45, but it is still referred to as a Colt 1911.

4. The spelling of the words for the verse quoted are from a 1557 Geneva Bible and are representative of the spelling style used at the time the Geneva Bible was in print.

QUESTION #82

The New Testament of the Geneva Bible was first published in 1557. The complete Geneva Bible was published in 1560. The last edition printed was in 1644. There are several differences in these continued editions. For example, John 3:16 which we just quoted from the "1599" doesn't read the same in the original 1557 Geneva New Testament. It reads like this:

John 3:16, 1557 GB - For God so loueth the world, that he hath geuen his only begotten Sonne, that none that beleue in him, should peryshe, but haue euerlasting lyfe.

Why didn't the proponents of the "1599" reproduce the 1557 "original" Geneva Bible? If that wasn't suitable, why didn't they use the final edition of 1644 as the Geneva Bible in its purest form and reproduce it? The answer is embarrassingly simple. The "1599" was the most convenient to do because it had already been done in 2003 by L. L. Brown. It was no purest desire to reproduce the perfect word of God. They simply reproduced the most available edition. If L. L. Brown had reproduced either the 1557 or 1644 or any edition in between, then the proponents of the Geneva Bible would have simply heralded that one as the "Bible that changed the world." They don't **care** about the Geneva Bible. They **care** about getting Bible believers to use something other than the King James Bible.

One of the reasons the recent Geneva Bible cannot be a true 1599 is revealed in this simple statement, made on page xx of the Introduction, "We have also changed the spelling of proper names in the Bible to that of the NKJV." In case you didn't get that I'll quote it again, "We have also changed the spelling of proper names in the Bible to that of the NKJV."

Now, how can it be a 1599 if it changes the spelling of proper names to those of a bible printed in 1982?

One of the clearest testimonies of the new Geneva Bible is found on page xxiv where it is referred to as, "This 2006 edition of the 1599 version of the Geneva Bible..."

On page xxv are recorded these words, "The 2006 edition of the 1599 Geneva version goes a step further; while keeping the Bible text and notes accurate word-for-word with the 16th- century edition, spelling has been updated and the type reset in an even easier-to-read form."

In 2008 I read the so-called 1599 Geneva Bible and wrote a book pointing out the many problems with it. Following are a few highlights from that work.

Observation #1 - Job 11:6

King James Bible

Job 11:6 - And that he would shew thee the secrets of wisdom, that they are double to that which is! Know therefore that God exacteth of thee less than thine iniquity deserveth.

2006 Geneva Bible

Job 11:6 - That he might show thee the secrets of wisdom how thou hast deserved double, according to right: know therefore that God hath forgotten thee for thine iniquity.

Observation #2 - Isa. 26:3

King James Bible

Isa. 26:3 - Thou wilt keep him in perfect peace, whose mind is stayed on thee: because he trusteth in thee.

2006 Geneva Bible

Isa. 26:3 - By an assured purpose wilt thou preserve perfect peace, because they trusted in thee.

Observation #3 - 1 Pet. 1:25
King James Bible

1 Pet. 1:25 - But the word of the Lord endureth for ever. And this is the word which by the gospel is preached unto you.

2006 Geneva Bible

1 Pet. 1:25 - But the word of the Lord endureth forever: and this is the word which is preached unto you.

It will be noted that the words by the gospel are not in the 2006 Geneva Bible. How does this line up with the other early English translations?

Wycliff	Omitted
Tyndale	Included
Cramner	Included
Great	Included
Geneva, 1557	Included
Geneva, 1560	Omitted
Bishops'	Included

Problems

Problem #1 - Gen. 22:8 - God will provide himself a lamb

In the King James Bible Genesis 22:8 reads, And Abraham said, My son, **God will provide himself a lamb** for a burnt offering: so they went both of them together. (Emphasis mine.) This is plainly a prophetic reference to Jesus Christ, the Lamb of God. How do we know? Because God **never** provided a **lamb** in the passage. Instead He provided a **ram**, leaving the prophecy approximately 1,900 years to be fulfilled by the crucifixion of Jesus Christ. The wording of the King James Bible is sublime in its shaded reference to God providing **Himself** the very sacrifice He was asking of Abraham.

The Geneva Bible does not contain this prophecy as it reads, "And Abraham answered, My son, **God will provide him a lamb** for a burnt offering: so they went both together." (Emphasis mine.) In the Geneva Bible the inference is nothing more than God providing a lamb for Himself, rather than God **being** the Lamb.

Three modern versions treat the text the same way as the Geneva translators did. The New International Version says, God himself will provide... while both the New American Standard Version and the New King James Version read very similar to the Geneva with, God will provide a lamb for himself...

Thus the 1599/2006 Geneva Bible agrees with three corrupt modern versions in deleting a prophetic reference to the crucifixion of Jesus Christ. **That's** a problem!

Problem #2 - Num. 23:21 - Double negative

Hired to curse Israel in Numbers chapter twenty-two, the prophet Balaam instead blesses Israel at the direction of the LORD. In Num. 23:21 we have a beautiful picture of how God looks at what we would consider a wayward people, He hath not beheld iniquity in Jacob, neither hath he seen perverseness in Israel: the LORD his God is with him, and the shout of a king is among them.

In Numbers 23:21 the Geneva Bible displays what is clearly an error in translation when it inserts a double negative into the verse making Balaam say the exact opposite of what God wanted him to say. The double negatives will be in bold type for easy comparison.

Num. 23:21 (GB) "He seeth none iniquity in Jacob, **nor** seeth **no** transgression in Israel: the LORD his God *is* with him, and the joyful shout of a King *is* among them."

By saying "**nor** seeth **no** transgression" the Geneva Bible has Balaam saying that God doesn't see "no transgression," meaning God **does see** transgression in Israel. This is plainly an error in translation and alters the meaning 180 degrees from what it was meant to say.

Problem #3 - 2 Sam. 21:19 - Who killed Goliath?

Anyone who has ever pointed out the errors of modern versions has eventually come to 2 Samuel 21:19 where the King James Bible reads, And there was again a battle in Gob with the Philistines, where Elhanan the son of Jaareoregim, a Bethlehemite, slew *the brother of* Goliath the Gittite, the staff of whose spear was like a weaver's beam.

It is to be noted that the words *the brother of* are in italics. Modern day critics of the King James Bible **love** to rail on the italicized words in the King James Bible as though no other translation ever added a single word to a verse in order that the end product would make sense. **All translations add words!** The Geneva Bible, the King James Bible, the New King James Version and the New American Standard Version put the added words in italics. Other versions also add words but simply don't italicize them.

Many modern versions delete the words, *the brother of* in verse 19, thus producing a bible with a contradiction: in 1 Sam 17 it says **David** killed Goliath while here in 2 Samuel 21 it says **Elhahan** killed Goliath.

Unfortunately, it seems that those corrupt modern versions are simply following the lead of the 1599/2006 Geneva Bible which reads, And there was yet another battle in Gob with the Philistines, where Elhanan the son of Jaare-Oregim, a Bethlehemite slew Goliath the Gittite, the staff of whose spear was like a weaver's beam.

Thus, the Geneva Bible contains a contradiction in it. The King James Bible has none.

Problem #4 - Ps. 23:5 - "presence" or "sight"

Psalm 23 is one the most well known portions of Scripture in the world. Christians and non-Christians around the world acknowledge its beauty and appreciate its sentiment. We will be looking at two verses in this psalm.

In the **King James Bible** Psalm 23:5 says, Thou preparest a table before me **in the presence of mine enemies:** thou anointest my head with oil; my cup runneth over. (Emphasis mine.)

In the **2006 Geneva Bible** the verse reads, Thou dost prepare a table before me **in the sight of mine adversaries:** thou dost anoint my head with oil, and my cup runneth over. (Emphasis mine.)

I am willing to accept the charge of "nit-picking" by the advocates of the 2006 Geneva Bible, but there is a great difference between "in the presence" and "in the sight." You can be a half-mile away and be "in the sight" of your enemies. They may **wish** to do you harm and simply cannot because they are too far away. But "in the presence" means they are **right there** and yet withheld from hurting you. That's a great difference and the Geneva Bible simply falls short. Other than the New English Bible, which reads like the GB, even most modern versions got it right.

Problem #5 - Ps. 23:6 - How long?

The last verse of Psalm 23 is familiar to most people, as it reads, Surely goodness and mercy shall follow me all the days of my life: and **I will dwell in the house of the LORD for ever.** (Emphasis mine.)

In the 2006 Geneva Bible this verse reads, Doubtless kindness and mercy shall follow me all the days of my life, and **I shall remain a long season in the house of the LORD.** (Emphasis mine.)

Now how long would **you** like to remain in the house of the LORD?

Problem #6 - Ps. 138:2 - An attack on the authority of Scripture

Most Bible believers have committed Ps. 138:2 to memory, I will worship toward thy holy temple, and praise thy name for thy lovingkindness and for thy truth: for **thou hast magnified thy word above all thy name.** (Emphasis mine.)

This verse reveals how high God holds His own word. Philippians 2:9-11 tells us that **every** knee shall bow and **every** tongue shall confess that Jesus Christ is Lord. This passage tells us how high God holds the name of His only-begotten Son. Then Psalm 138:2 reveals that God upholds His word even higher than that! A magnificent revelation of how God values Scripture.

Unfortunately, in the Geneva Bible this exaltation of the written word evaporates like a drop of water on hot asphalt. It reads, I will worship toward thine holy Temple and praise thy Name, because of thy loving-kindness and for thy truth: for **thou hast magnified thy Name above all things by thy word.** (Emphasis mine.)

Problem #7 - Zech. 9:9 - "and saved himself"?

In the Bible Zech. 9:9 reads, Rejoice greatly, O daughter of Zion; shout, O daughter of Jerusalem: behold, thy King cometh unto thee: he is just, **and having salvation;** lowly, and riding upon an ass, and upon a colt the foal of an ass. (Emphasis mine.)

Although the Old Testament Jews missed it, we now know this is a prophetic reference to Jesus Christ entering Jerusalem on the back of an ass's foal and **bringing salvation** with Him.

This great truth is not found in the 2006 Geneva Bible which reads in Zech. 9:9, Rejoice greatly, O daughter of Zion: shout for joy, O daughter Jerusalem: behold, thy king cometh unto thee: he is just, **and saved himself,** poor and riding upon an ass, and upon a colt the foal of an ass.

Not only does this errant translation eliminate the bringing of salvation to all who believe but it inserts in the text of Scripture another contradiction. It says He "saved himself" which is the **one thing** Jesus **didn't** do. As the song says, "He could have called ten thousand angels," but instead chose to freely give Himself a sacrifice for our sins. The Geneva Bible is greatly in error here.

Problem #8 - Zech. 11:12 - It wasn't "my wages."

In the King James Bible Zech. 11:12 states, And I said unto them, If ye think good, give me **my price;** and if not, forbear. So they weighed for **my price** thirty pieces of silver. (Emphasis mine.)

Again, unbeknownst to those of Old Testament times, this was a prophetic reference to the amount of money Jesus' betrayer would receive for his treachery.

Not so in the Geneva Bible which renders Zech. 11:12 to read, And I said unto them, If ye think it good, give me **my wages:** and if no, leave off: so they weighed for **my wages** thirty pieces of silver. (Emphasis mine.)

Thirty pieces of silver was **the price** paid to betray Jesus Christ. It was not His "wages." Another error in the Geneva Bible.

Problem #9 - Mal. 2:16 - Say what!?

Fundamentalists are in love with Mal. 2:16 because it gives them authority to openly try to drive many preachers from the ministry due to their "lack of qualification." The verse reads, For the LORD, the God of Israel, saith that **he hateth putting away:** for one covereth violence with his garment, saith the LORD of hosts: therefore take heed to your spirit, that ye deal not treacherously. (Emphasis mine.)

I'm sure they'll be pleased with the rendition found in the Geneva Bible, **If thou hatest her, put her away,** saith the Lord God of Israel... (Emphasis mine.)

Ah...yes, well I guess that verse will be the text for many a sermon!

Problem #10 - John 1:3 - "it," the Creator

In John 1:1 we are introduced to Jesus as both "the Word" and the Creator. Then in verse three we are told, All things were made by him; and without him was not any thing made that was made.

The Geneva Bible renders this, All things were made by **it**, and without **it** was made nothing that was made.

How do the early English translations render this passage?

Wycliff	him
Tyndale	it
Cramner	it
Great	it
Geneva, 1557	it
Geneva, 1560	it
Bishops’	it

Why did I include this information when most early English translations agreed with the 2006 Geneva Bible? I wanted you to see the **superiority** of the King James Bible over **all** its predecessors!

Problem #11 - Acts 1:18 - Judas, hanged or fallen?

In the King James Bible Acts 1:18 reads, Now this man purchased a field with the reward of iniquity; and falling headlong, he burst asunder in the midst, and all his bowels gushed out.

The Geneva Bible says, He therefore hath purchased a field with the reward of iniquity: and when he had thrown down himself headlong, he brast asunder in the midst, and all his bowels gushed out.

In Matthew 27:5 we are told that Judas, following his betrayal of Christ, went and hanged himself. It is then obvious that, while his body was hanging the earthquake occurred during Christ’s crucifixion and either the limb or the rope broke and Judas’ body fell headlong, he burst asunder in the midst, and all his bowels gushed out.

The 2006 Geneva Bible, like the King James, says he hanged himself in Matthew. But the wording of Acts 1:18 creates a contradiction as it then claims he threw himself off a cliff to kill himself. The King James rendering of Acts 1:18

allows no contradiction. How does this line up with the other early English translations?

Wycliff	and he was hanged, and to brast the middle
Tyndale	when he was hanged, brast a sunder in the mids
Cramner	when he was hanged, he burst a sunder in the mids
Great	when he was hanged, he burst a sunder in the mids
Geneva, 1557	when he killed him self, he brast a sunder in the mids
Geneva, 1560	when he had thrown down himself head longs he brast a sunder in the mids
Bishops'	when he was hanged, he burst asunder in the mids

So we see that all early English translations, except the Geneva, protect the text from contradiction. The 1557, though weak, could be said not to cause a contradiction, but the 1560 and the 2006 (1599) both create a problem that isn't there.

Problem #12 - Acts 12:4 - No "Easter"

Everyone knows that in Acts 12:4 the King James Bible says, And when he had apprehended him, he put him in prison, and delivered him to four quaternions of soldiers to keep him; intending after **Easter** to bring him forth to the people. (Emphasis mine.)

It is plain from verse three, Then were the days of unleavened bread, that Peter was arrested during the Days of Unleavened Bread which occur Abib 15-21 (Lev.23:4, 5), which is **after** the passover on Abib 14. Therefore the passover was already past when Herod made his statement. But the pagan festival of Easter could fall anytime between

March 22 and April 25. Thus the **pagan holiday** of Easter was yet to come at the time of Peter's arrest. Therefore it is obvious that Herod planned on waiting until **that** date.

Critics of the King James Bible have actually tried to use this verse as an example of mistranslation. They say that the word "pascha" should have been translated "passover." They try to convince their listeners that the word "passover" in Scripture includes all eight days from Abib 14 to the 21st. There are numerous problems with this view, **all of them presented in Scripture**. Rather than review **all** of the biblical evidence we will look at two irrefutable testimonies that the "passover," when referred to in Scripture, is only **one day**, Abib 14.

Numbers 33:3 And they departed from Rameses in the first month, on the fifteenth day of the first month; on the morrow after the passover the children of Israel went out with an high hand in the sight of all the Egyptians. This reference **plainly tells the reader that Abib 15 is officially, in God's eyes, AFTER** the passover. To choose to believe anything else is to choose to believe something that is anti-scriptural. (That's called heresy.)

In **Matthew 26:18** Jesus said, And he said, Go into the city to such a man, and say unto him, The Master saith, My time is at hand; **I will keep the passover** at thy house with my disciples.

Now **you** are faced with two choices:

1. Jesus kept an **eight day feast** and was then betrayed. Of course, the Scripture does not teach this. It says He was arrested that very night, right after He kept what is now known as The Last Supper which should more properly be called The Last Passover.

2. Jesus kept the **first night** of an eight day feast and was taken, "in the same night," and crucified having **never kept the entire passover** even though that is what He **said** He was going to do. Thus, if the passover referred to in Scripture is eight days long, Jesus was wrong. **God** made a mistake! Since Bible believers don't believe there are mistakes in the Bible, nor in our Lord, we accept the **biblical truth** that the Passover was one day (Abib 14), the Days of Unleavened Bread are the seven immediately after the Passover (Abib 15-21) and Jesus was **God**, therefore He was never wrong or mistaken.

To change "Easter" to "passover" is to insert an error into Scripture where there was none before. That is exactly what the translators of the 1599/ 2006 Geneva Bible did when they translated Acts 12:4 as, And when he had caught him, he put him in prison, and delivered him to four quaternions of soldiers to be kept, intending after the **Passover** to bring him forth to the people.

To do this they had to ignore the testimony of almost every early English translation. Following is their testimony.

Wycliff	"pask"
Tyndale	"ester"
Cramner	"Ester"
Great	"Ester"
Geneva, 1557	"Easter"
Geneva, 1560	"Passover"
Bishops'	"Easter"

It is sad to see that, once again, the 1599/2006 Geneva Bible parts company with its much more accurate ancestor, the 1557 Geneva Bible.

Problem #13 - Heb. 10:12 - A postmillenial comma.

In the King James Bible Heb. 10:12 states, But this man, after hc had offered one sacrifice for sins for ever, sat down on the right hand of God; Yes, I have made the comma **bold**. It is the subject of the next problem with the Geneva Bible.

In the 2006 Geneva Bible the verse reads, But this man after he had offered one sacrifice for sins, sitteth forever at the right hand of God,

The wording of the two versions is almost identical. It is the position of the comma that changes the meaning radically. There is a great difference between, "offered one sacrifice for sins for ever," and ", sitteth forever at the right hand of God,"

The King James Bible makes it plain that Jesus Christ offered one sacrifice for sins which never again has to be repeated, and afterwards sat down at the right hand of God where He waits until His future return to earth. By relocating the comma the translators of the 2006 Geneva Bible have the Lord making His sacrifice and then **sitting forever** at the right hand of God. He is **never** coming back! This is an error and contrary to numerous other Scripture which plainly foretell His return.

How do the early English translations stack up?

Wycliff	places the comma like the Authorized Version
Tyndale	places the comma like the 2006 Geneva Bible
Cramner	places the comma like the 2006 Geneva Bible
Great	places the comma like the 2006 Geneva Bible
Geneva, 1557	places the comma like the 2006 Geneva Bible
Geneva, 1560	places the comma like the 2006 Geneva Bible
Bishops'	places the comma like the 2006 Geneva Bible

Once again we see that the majority doesn't always rule! To place the comma where most of the early English translations did is to insert a contradiction into the text. If for no other reason than it said Jesus "sitteth forever at the right hand of God," yet we read in Acts 7:55 that Stephen saw Jesus **standing** on the Father's right hand. Wycliff got it right. Then correct punctuation was sidetracked until 1611. It's the difference between "good" translations and a **perfect** one.

Problem #14 - 1 John 2:23 - Where's the rest of the verse?

In the King James Bible 1 John 2:23 reads, Whosoever denieth the Son, the same hath not the Father: *he that acknowledgeth the Son hath the Father also.* It is to be noted that the entire last half of the verse is in italics. The reason is simple. The King James Bible was translated from the Textus Receptus and the Textus Receptus does not contain the last half of 1 John 2:23. The King James translators added the words from the Latin, and since they had no Greek authority for the passage they put them in italics. (Honest chaps!) It was years later that a fourth century Greek manuscript was discovered that contained the entire verse just as it is in the King James Bible. (Prophetic chaps!)

All three Geneva editions read, Whosoever denieth the Son, the same hath not the Father. omitting the rest of the verse.

The early English translations translated the verse in agreement with:

Wycliff	King James Bible
Tyndale	Geneva Bible
Cramner	King James Bible
Great	King James Bible
Bishops'	King James Bible

It should be noted here that this is a good example of why you want to be a King James Man not a Textus Receptus Man. Many men, lacking the true faith to believe God could really preserve His words and give us a copy today, but afraid their lack of faith will be discovered, scurry to the Textus Receptus and declare **it** the "preserved word of God," **not knowing that there is NO word-for-word translation of the Textus Receptus anywhere in English!** So what do you do now? Deny the Greek or deny the English? The King James Bible may be 99% the Textus Receptus but it is 100% **correct**!

Thus, although the Geneva Bible is a child of the Textus Receptus it, like the other pre-King James Bibles, was a pretty good effort but not the perfect word of God. It might be noted that many of our charges against modern translations first saw the light of day in the Geneva.

Oh, and in case you're interested in the **truth**, in the museum at Plymouth Colony there is a King James Bible which was printed in 1620, the year of the Mayflower's voyage, which belonged to one of the most famous colonists known, John Alden. Would you like to see it? Go to: https://manifoldgreatness.wordpress.com/2011/11/22/the-first-king-james-bible-in-america/

Question #83

Question: Isn't the King James Bible written in Old English?

Answer: No, but that is a common misconception.

Explanation: Because of the presence of words like "thee" and "thou" and "thy" and "thine" people mistakenly believe that the King James Bible is written in Old English. Unfortunately, some less than well-meaning critics of the KJB are more than happy to promote that myth even if they know it not to be true.

The English language came into being in three distinct phases. Anyone who speaks Modern English today would find Old English impossible to read and Middle English just as difficult. They may slightly recognize a word or two that seem similar to the Modern English we speak today but reading it would be no different than trying to read a foreign language. English developed in three segments:

Old English: 449 AD - 1100 AD
Middle English: 1100 AD - 1450 AD
Modern English: 1450 AD - Present

The following will demonstrate the vast differences between these three stages of development.

A. Old English: 450-1100 AD - Below is an example of Old English taken from *The Anglo-Saxon*

Chronicle, written in 1066 AD, just before Middle English came into being.

Example #1

"An. M.LXVI. On þyssum geare man halgode þet mynster æt Westmynstre on Cyldamæsse dæg 7 se cyng Eadward forðferde on Twelfts mæsse æfen 7 hine mann bebyrgede on Twelftan mæssedæg innan þære niwa halgodre circean on Westmyntr"

It is plain to see that Old English is as impossible for English-speakers of our day to understand as it is for them to understand words written in a foreign language. Below is the Modern English translation of the above Old English quote.

"1066 In this year the monastery at Westminster was hallowed on Childermas day (28 December). And king Eadward died on Twelfth-mass eve (5 January) and he was buried on Twelfth-mass day, in the newly hallowed church at Westminster."

Example #2

"Fæder ure þu þe eart on heofonum, Si þin nama gehalgod. To becume þin rice, gewurþe ðin willa, on eorðan swa swa on heofonum. Urne gedæghwamlican hlaf syle us todæg, and forgyf us ure gyltas, swa swa we forgyfað urum gyltendum. And ne gelæd þu us on costnunge, ac alys us of yfele. Soþlice."

You may not know it but you just read the portion of scripture in Matthew, chapter 6, that is known as The Lord's Prayer. but, because it was written in Old English it is impossible to understand. The King James Bible was not written in Old English.

B. Middle English: 1100-1450 AD - Modern English-speakers would fare no better in trying to decipher anything written in Middle English as the example below will illustrate. See how well you do interpreting this example of Middle English.

Lauerd me steres, noght wante sal me:
In stede of fode þare me louked he.
He fed me ouer watre ofe fode,
Mi saule he tornes in to gode.
He led me ouer sties of rightwisenes,
For his name, swa hali es.
For, and ife .I. ga in mid schadw ofe dede,
For þou wiþ me erte iuel sal .i. noght drede;
Þi yherde, and þi stafe ofe mighte,
Þai ere me roned dai and nighte.
Þou graiþed in mi sighte borde to be,
Ogaines þas þat droued me;
Þou fatted in oli me heued yhite;
And mi drinke dronkenand while schire es ite!
And filigh me sal þi mercy
Alle daies ofe mi life for-þi;
And þat .I. wone in hous ofe lauerd isse
In lengþe of daies al wiþ blisse

So, other than "For his name" and a few words like "dai" (day) and "nighte" (night), how did you do? You saw several words which looked familiar to you but you probably failed to realize you were reading the 23rd Psalm! The King James Bible was not written in Middle English.

C. Modern English came into being around 1450 AD and has been with us ever since. Thus you see that, in spite of those "thee's" and "thou's" and the strange spellings for words like "son" (sonne) and "evil" (euille) that are found in its original type-setting, the King James Bible is one of the first Bibles written in Modern English, not Old nor Middle English.

But, even though the English we call Modern basically began around 1450 it did not solidify until the 17th Century, meaning it was too unstable to represent the perfect word of God. Here's why:

1. Capitalization - In the early days of Modern English capitalization was done at the whim of the writer. (Read any part of the journals of Lewis & Clark [1803] and you will see that even at this late date capitalization was capricious.)

2. Spelling - Also, in early Modern English spelling was determined by whatever the writer chose it to be. In fact, the word "said" is spelled four different ways in the same volume of an original King James Bible!

a. Gen. 48:18 - "saide"
b. Gen. 48:19 - "said"
c. Jud. 19:8 - "sayd"
d. I Sam. 15:15 - "sayde"

Yet it is plain to any reader that all four times the word in question is "said." (Remember, God promised to preserve the WORDS of Scripture, not the letters.)

3. Grammatical changes - While the former two points are not deal breakers, the third might be. Around the end of the 16th Century there were grammatical changes that advanced English and helped usher in Modern English as we know it. This solidifying effected several areas of English, including:

QUESTION #83

a. Pronouns - Changes that agree with our Modern English usage rather than the archaic Old & Middle English occurred about the beginning of the 17th Century.

b. Vowel shifting - The pronunciation of vowels changed between Middle & Modern English. Although what we would consider the modern spelling of a word would be used the way in which it was pronounced changed from Middle to Modern English.

	Middle English	**Modern English**
1. Sheep	"shape"	"sheep"
2. Doom	"dome"	"doom"
3. Boat	"boot"	"boat"
4. Life	"lafe"	"life"

c. New word additions - The English language was rapidly expanding in influence and geography. It was soon to supplant German, French and even Latin as the world's universal language. To do so it incorporated words from these languages to better communicate. The rest is history.

Question #84

Question: I have a King James Bible that has a word misspelled in it. How can it be the "preserved word of God" if it has a word misspelled?

Answer: That isn't a valid issue.

Explanation: That is, unfortunately, a printing error which does not reflect on God's promise of preservation, since there are countless printings with the word properly spelled.

I have an New American Standard Version with a similar printing error which spells "witness" as "witess" in one place, but I never use it as a reason. to criticize the NASV. There are enough legitimate **translational** problems with the NASV. No one needs to condemn it for a printing error.

Question #85

Question: We had a "King James Bible believer" preaching at our church and he showed that some King James Bibles say "fats" in Joel 3:13, and some say "vats" and that everyone who had a "vats" Bible didn't have a **real** King James Bible. Is this so?

Answer: Your church was subjected to a con job by a money-seeking con-man who doesn't care if he leaves church members fighting among each other as long as **he** gets a check for his ministry.

Explanation: When a man spends hours and hours studying his Bible it shows in his preaching and teaching. There is no substitute for time spent reading and studying the word of God. Their preaching and teaching is filled with little nuggets of Bible information that generally impress and edify his hearers.

No one notices and covets this more than proud, lazy preachers. These men desire the accolades but have no intention of spending the time in Bible study that produces powerful preaching. Lazy preachers have found a way to impress their listeners without losing any of their precious golf time. They resort to Preaching Pyrotechnics.

Everybody likes fireworks. So, rather than give their hearers any **meat** from the word of God they seek out something sensational that will bring "ooh's" and "aah's."

There is no substance, just flash and noise and a dazzling performance. This "fats" versus "vats" controversy is just that, no Bible truth, just flash and noise. But when they're finished with their money-making performance, they take their check and blow town leaving behind them Christians who got along fine before they showed up now at each others' throats over who does or doesn't have a "real" King James Bible.

If you think I'm making this up, I have a pastor friend who took one of these con-men out for coffee and asked him point blank, "Why do you do that? It leaves my people fighting with each other."

Revealing how little he cares for God's people as long as he gets a check he said, "Oh, I only do that to raise money for our Bible printing ministry."

But, condemnation of charlatans aside, how **do** we explain the "fats/vats" controversy? Well, the con-job only works where well-meaning Christians make an errant assumption about the preservation of God's words. It happens because of a phenomenon I call, Conviction Poker. Here's how Conviction Poker works. A shallow, overzealous Christian will hear about a conviction another Christian has and basically say, "I'll see your conviction and raise you a conviction." The spirit of this game is, "Oh, you think **you** believe the Bible? Well I believe even more than you do!" so when someone states that they believe "every word" of the King James Bible these zealots will respond with, "You believe the **words?** Why I go farther than that. I even believe the **letters!**" ("I'll see your 'words' and raise you the 'letters'.")

When you ask most Christians what the smallest unit of preservation is they suddenly get a pious look on their faces and solemnly retort, "A jot and a tittle." Many think, "I'll see your 'jot & tittle' and raise you a classier statement." Then they respond, "Why a 'jot' is like the dot of an 'i' and a 'tittle' is like the cross of a 't'. **That's how thoroughly God promised to preserve his words!!!!!!!"** While this makes for great theatrics and is a "dramatic" stand to take it is both misleading and wrong.

Why is it misleading? Because a "jot" is an entire Hebrew letter. The dot of an "i" is only a portion of a letter. The same thing is true concerning a tittle. A "tittle" is an entire Hebrew letter. The cross of a "t" is only a portion of a letter. So this big, bad, chest-beating description is misleading. And the one doing the misleading should know better.

But the "jot & tittle" teaching is wrong because letters are not the smallest unit God promised to preserve. God said the "jots & tittles" would in no wise pass from the law, till all be fulfilled. (Matt. 5:18) This statement pertains **only to the Law** not the entire sacred text of Scripture. Why the Law? Because Jesus **fulfilled** the Law thus allowing the jots and tittles to pass away. (**Read the verse!**)

The smallest unit of preservation that God promised is a **word**, not a letter:

Psalm 12:6 The **words** of the LORD are pure **words:** as silver tried in a furnace of earth, purified seven times.
7 Thou shalt keep **them,** O LORD, thou shalt preserve **them** from this generation for ever.

Proverbs 30:6 Add thou not unto his **words,** lest he reprove thee, and thou be found a liar.

Matthew 24:35 Heaven and earth shall pass away, but my **words** shall not pass away.

QUESTION #85

Revelation 22:19 And if any man shall take away from the **words** of the book of this prophecy, God shall take away his part out of the book of life, and out of the holy city, and from the things which are written in this book.

God promised to preserve His **WORDS**, not the **letters** no matter how spiritual it makes a preacher sound to boast about "jots" and "tittles!"

We will examine the spelling, pronunciations and variations these con-men[5] use.

1. "fats" vs. **"vats"** in the Book of Joel:
Joel 2:24 And the floors shall be full of wheat, and the **fats** shall overflow with wine and oil.

Joel 3:13 Put ye in the sickle, for the harvest is ripe: come, get you down; for the press is full, the **fats** overflow; for their wickedness is great.

The con-man reads one, or both, of the verses in Joel from a Bible (**that he prints!**) that reads "fats." He then asks for a raise of hands of all who have a King James Bible that reads "vats." He then informs all those with a Bible that says "vats" do not **really** have a **KING JAMES** Bible because that word was changed by greedy (Hmm?) publishing companies

---

5. Many preachers have heard this false teaching and, having not studied it thoroughly, ignorantly repeated it because seems like such a strong stand for preservation of the Bible. These are not con-men, they are simply misled. The con-men do it to get money!

who changed the words rather than by sanctified, holy printing press in a church basement.[6]

But wait! Do you know what a wine **fat** is? It's a wine **vat!** That's right, it's the same thing spelled two different ways.[7] You could at **a picture** of one and say, "Oh look, a wine fat," and someone could respond, "Yep, that's a wine vat all right." There is no difference but the spelling.

2. "houghed" vs. **"hocked"**

Joshua 11:9 And Joshua did unto them as the LORD bade him: he **houghed** their horses, and burnt their chariots with fire.

2 Samuel 8:4 And David took from him a thousand chariots, and seven hundred horsemen, and twenty thousand footmen: and David **houghed** all the chariot horses, but reserved of them for an hundred chariots.

After visiting Joel, the con-man will lead his marks to either Joshua or 2 Samuel or both and ask how many people have a "King James" Bible that reads "hocked" (pronounced

---

6. Please understand I am **not** against churches printing Bibles. I think it is wonderful. I am against using trickery to get the money to print those Bibles. I am against someone who brings **division** into a church to their own profit, not caring if they leave behind a church in turmoil.

7. At this point someone will righteously declare, "Gipp is for these publishing companies that change spelling!" Actually I'm not. In fact I wouldn't trust **any** publishing company that said they were going to print a King James Bible with updated spelling because I **know** none of them truly believe in a perfect Bible on this earth and therefore **I don't trust them!**

"hok") instead of "houghed" (pronounced "hewed"). He then repeats his charge that the "hocked" Bibles are all corrupt. (But he's willing t sell them a **real** King James Bible of which he just happens to have a supply.)

I stumbled onto the resolution for this teaching while reading an article about the early aviation industry. In 1912 Allan Loughead and his brother Malcolm Loughead, both Scots, founded an aircraft manufacturing company and named it, Loughead Aircraft Manufacturing Company. The company failed in 1920. Then in 1926 Allan decided to have another try at building airplanes, but to prevent the mispronunciation of his last name decided to spell it **phonetically** and **Lockheed** Aircraft Company was born.

Allan Loughead's last name which Americans would pronounce, "Low head" was **actually** pronounced "Lockheed" in his native Scotland. Thus "lough" isn't to be pronounced "low" but "lock."

In the same manner "hough" is not to be pronounced "hew" but "hock." You may doubt this but check a Webster's 1828 dictionary. While this book came into existence over 200 years after the King James Bible and is **not** our **final** authority, it **is** a definitive authority of the English language. If you look up the word "hock," you will find its pronunciation in parentheses. Thus you will see: hock (hok). If you then look up "hough" you will find this: hough (hok). Both words are pronounced the same because both words **are** the same.

If you want to see "hewed" in the Bible then you should check **Deuteronomy 10:3,** And I made an ark of shittim wood, and **hewed** two tables of stone like unto the first, and went up into the mount, having the two tables in mine hand.

3. "throughly" vs. **"thoroughly"**

2 Timothy 3:17 That the man of God may be perfect, **throughly** furnished unto all good works.

I once heard a young preacher say that "throughly" is different than "thoroughly." He then said that "throughly" was like looking through clear glass. Well if that's true it doesn't fit the verse at all!

But the sad fact is that he **made up** the definition of throughly for the simple reason that he wanted to condemn any King James Bible that said, "thoroughly." He had to manufacture "facts" to prove something that simply isn't real. This is dishonest.

Think about it, if the police searched a house they would search it "thoroughly" and it could also be said it had been searched "throughly." No, **no, NO! I am not** defending or justifying any Bible printer who claims they updated words in their edition of the King James Bible. I am saying that there is no difference between "throughly" and "thoroughly." Of course, those playing Conviction Poker will disagree with what I say because... **they have to defend their actions!**

Let's try to approach this with some honesty and integrity. No one wants to sit and listen to a minister preach who doesn't know much about the Book from which he is preaching. Verse seventeen **cannot** be examined independently of verse sixteen.

2 Timothy 3:16 All scripture is given by inspiration of God, and is profitable for doctrine, for reproof, for correction, for instruction in righteousness:

So 2 Timothy 3:16 says God inspired Scripture to be

used to teach doctrine, reprove error, show what correct actions are and for instruction in righteousness. Verse sixteen tells **what is to be done with Scripture** and verse seventeen tells **who is to be carrying out** the duty list of verse sixteen. Thus, Scripture was given to **arm the Man of God** to **accomplish the duty of God.** Thus the Man of God may be thoroughly furnished to all good works.

4. "ensample" vs. **"example"**

I have been told (very solemnly, I might add) that an "example" is something you **do** but and **"ensample"** is something you sample as in tasting. I don't mean to mess up a poetic-sounding sermon but this is a **manufactured** definition. How do I know? I looked up "ensample" in the dictionary and it had a **one word** definition, "example." But it pointed out that both ensample and example were introduced in Middle English around 1200 AD from the French word "essample." But the French got it from the Latin, "exemplum." **All four words mean "example!"**

Both "ensample" and "example" are exclusive to the New Testament. "Ensample" appears just three times and "example," eight. Rather than pick one or two of these eleven references I will simply reprint all of them below.

Ensample vs. **Example**
Ensample:

Phil. 3:17 Brethren, be followers together of me, and mark them which walk so as ye have us for an **ensample.**

2 Thes. 3:9 Not because we have not power, but to make ourselves an **ensample** unto you to follow us.

2 Peter 2:6 And turning the cities of Sodom and Gomorrha into ashes condemned them with an overthrow, making them an **ensample** unto those that after should live ungodly;

Try replacing **"ensample"** with "taste" and see what you get.

Example:

Matt. 1:19 Then Joseph her husband, being a just man, and not willing to make her a publick **example**, was minded to put her away privily.

John 13:15 For I have given you an **example**, that ye should do as I have done to you.

1 Tim. 4:12 Let no man despise thy youth; but be thou an **example** of the believers, in word, in conversation, in charity, in spirit, in faith, in purity.

Heb. 4:11 Let us labour therefore to enter into that rest, lest any man fall after the same **example** of unbelief.

Heb. 8:5 Who serve unto the **example** and shadow of heavenly things, as Moses was admonished of God when he was about to make the tabernacle: for, See, saith he, that thou make all things according to the pattern shewed to thee in the mount.

James 5:10 Take, my brethren, the prophets, who have spoken in the name of the Lord, for an **example** of suffering affliction, and of patience.

QUESTION #85

1 Peter 2:21 For even hereunto were ye called: because Christ also suffered for us, leaving us an **example**, that ye should follow his steps:

Jude 1:7 Even as Sodom and Gomorrha, and the cities about them in like manner, giving themselves over to fornication, and going after strange flesh, are set forth for an **example**, suffering the vengeance of eternal fire.

Now, read all eleven references and be honest and you will see that there isn't one verse where "ensample" and "example" couldn't be used interchangeably. (Please also note that in the three uses of "ensample" no one is tasting anything!)

While this cheap, dishonest tactic is used only for the purpose of fleecing God's people, those poor listeners who believe it are being thrown into terrible confusion. (Who's the author of confusion?) If you say a King James Bible that has "vats" instead of "fats" and "hocked" instead of "houghed" isn't a **real** king James Bible because the spelling has been changed then some sharp King James Bible rejector is going to confront you by saying, "But **you** don't have a **real** King James Bible either because the original printing in 1611 spelled "son", "sonne" and "evil", "eville" and "been", "bene." So **you're using a 'corrupted'** King James Bible because the spelling in yours has been changed since 1611." **BOOM!** You were just entrapped by extending inspiration farther than God said it would go!

Here's just a partial list of words that have had their spelling changed from 1611 to today:

Reference	1611		Today
1. Jud. 16:8	bene dried	vs.	been dried
2. Isa 17:13	mountaines	vs.	mountains
3. John 3:16	Sonne	vs.	Son
4. John 3:16	ye	vs.	the
5. John 3:16	beleeveth	vs.	believeth
6. John 3:18	onely	vs.	only
7. Acts 7:6	seede	vs.	seed
8. Acts 7:6	euill	vs.	evil
9. Acts 7:6	foure	vs.	four
10. Acts 7:6	yeeres	vs.	years

At this point the truly shrewd will say, "OK, then I'll get a 1611 reprint and then I'll have the correct spelling." Sorry, you just jumped out of the frying pan and into a pit of quicksand!

Many Bible believers think that there were two King James Bibles collated by the translators in 1611. There weren't. There were three: One from the two companies of translators at Oxford University, one from the two companies of translators at Cambridge University, one from the two companies of translators at Westminster.

The following comparison comes from those three King James Bibles which **all** have "1611" on their title page. We will address them as A, B and C.

Reference	A	B	C
1. Gen 48:8	saide	sayde	sayd
2. Josh. 10:25	be dismaid	be dismayed	bee dismaid
3. I Sam 10:1	viall	violl	viol
4. I Kg. 2:11	raigned bee	reigned be	raigned be
5. 2 Kg. 10:9	Ye be	Yee bee	Yee be

6. Isa 30:26	shalbe	shall be	shal bee
7. Isa. 60:6	forth the praises:	foorth the praises	forth the prayses
8. Jer. 35:18	ye..all	yee...all	Yee...al
9. Ezek. 11:15	sayd; Get yee	said, Get ye	said, Get yee

Now, which 1611 King James Bible are you going to get. Don't worry, I already know the answer. You're going to get 1611 King James Bible "A." How do I know that? Because Thomas Nelson Publishers printed a facsimile of an original 1611 King James Bible in 1982 when they launched their New King James Version. Of the three represented the one they printed is King James Bible "A." When Thomas Nelson no longer had an interest in this 1611 reprint they sold the rights to Hendrickson Publishing who now prints it. Here's how the Hendrickson reprint compares to those above.

1611 Reprint (1982)

1. Gen. 48:8 - saide
2. Josh. 10:25 - be dismaid
3. I Sam. 10:1 - viall
4. I Kg. 2:11 - raigned bee
5. 2 Kg. 10:9 - Ye be
6. Pro. 24:6 - counsellers...safetie
7. Isa. 30:26 - shalbe
8. Isa. 60:6 - forth the praises
9. Jer. 35:18 - ye...all
10. Ezek. 11:15 - sayd; Get yee

But wait! It gets worse. Examine the Hendrickson 1611 Reprint and you will find that the word "said" is spelled four different ways!

1. Gen. 48:18 - saide
2. Gen. 48:19 - said
3. Jud. 19:8 - sayd
4. I Sam. 15:15 - sayde

In fact, this same edition spells the word "ye" two different ways in Ezra 8:29 where it reads , ye & yee.

Spelling was not uniform when the King James Bible was printed. But then, if you ever read anyone's letters from the early Nineteenth Century you will see that it wasn't even uniform by then.

I am sorry but at some point you are going to have to admit that the smallest unit of preservation is a **word**, not a letter, no matter how holy you think you sound talking about "jots" and "tittles."

For the third and final time let me say that I **am not** in favor of anyone printing an edition of the King James Bible with "updated spelling." Why do I accept the spelling changes we have today but am against anyone updating the spelling today? Because **I don't trust** today's modern Bible publishers. The spelling changes that were made to this point were done with a pure heart in an effort to unify the spelling. Every major Bible publishing company today is owned and operated by non-Bible believers, and, in some cases possibly by unsaved people. These people do not hold the Bible with the same reverence that born-again Bible believers do. In fact, most have a version that they have commissioned just to increase their revenue. They care little if they ever have to print another King James Bible. I'd sooner trust a Congressman than a modern Bible publisher!

So, although I **prefer** a King James Bible that says, "fats" and "houghed", those who have the **same words** spelled differently do not possess a "lesser" King James Bible. God doesn't seem to be concerned with how a word is spelled. We shouldn't make more of the subject than God does.

Question #86

Question: There are hundreds of English Bibles in print. How are we supposed to read them all and decide which is the real word of God?

Answer: There aren't hundreds of English Bibles. There are only two.

Explanation: I once did a thorough study of the number of Bibles published in English and arrived at 474 of them. The first was the Gospel of John, translated from Latin by the British monk, The Venerable Bede around 735AD. This translation and the next seven were translated into Old English which neither you nor I could read.

The ninth English translation consisted of portions of the Gospels which were translated from Latin around 1150AD. This translation, we'll call it #9, and the next seven were translated in Middle English, again, a variation of English we would not be able to read today. Among these eight Middle English scriptures is John Wycliff's translation of 1380. This is the translation that ignited a hunger among the English for a Bible in their language. It upset Roman Catholic officials because God's people had access to the words of God without the twisted teachings of the Roman Catholic Church.

This hunger for God's words ultimately led to the very first Bible translated into Modern English by William Tyndale in 1525. Tyndale's work opened the floodgates of truth and ultimately led to the world-changing King James Bible. Tyndale was arrested by Catholic officials and burned at the stake on October 6, 1536 for his "crime" of giving the English people the ability to possess the word of God in their native tongue.

But I said there were only **two** Bibles although I documented the existence of 474 in the English Language. If you subtract the first sixteen non-Modern English Bibles that leaves 458 in **our** readable style of the language. What gives? The answer is simple. **Every** Bible printed comes from one of only **two sources** of Greek manuscripts. They are either a translation of the good line of manuscripts that originate in Antioch, Syria, where the New Testament Church was located (Acts 11:19-29), or they are a translation of the corrupted manuscripts produced in Alexandria, Egypt, by men who did not believe the Bible to be divine and who rejected the great truths it teaches.

Today most modern translations are based on this flawed Greek text. A Brief list of the most well-known of these tainted translations is: Revised Version - 1881; American Standard Version - 1901; Revised Standard Version - 1952; New American Standard Version - 1960; Good News Bible - 1966; New English Bible - 1970; The Living Bible - 1971; New International Version - 1973; New Century Version - 1987; Contemporary English Version - 1995; New Revised Standard Version - 1999; English Standard Version - 2001; New English Translation - 2007; Holman Christian Standard Bible - 2009; Common English Bible - 2011; New Living Translation - 2015 and the Amplified Version - 2015.

QUESTION #86

Well-known translations from the Textus Receptus are the New King James Version - 1982, Modern English Version - 2014 and of course the King James Bible of 1611. Although the NKJV and MEV use a good Greek source, both are filtered through the corrupt Alexandrian Mentality with devastating effects. Basically the NKJV reproduced the errors found in the NASV while the MEV gravitates to the corruptions of the NIV and ESV.

So, although you may go into a Christian bookstore and see 30 or 40 English Bibles sporting different version names, you are actually only looking at **two** bibles, translated from two Greek Texts.

Question #87

Question: My Bible college professor said that the King James translators were sinners and that God couldn't use such men to preserve His holy words. Is that correct?

Answer: It is correct that they were sinners, but the charge that God couldn't use them to preserve His words is a fake charge which your professor doesn't even believe. He just uses it hoping to stump you and get you to abandon your faith in God's Perfect Bible.

Explanation: Since **nowhere in the Bible**, which is our final authority in all matters of faith and **practice**, does it say God can't use a sinner to preserve His words. Therefore this lame argument does not carry either the weight or authority of Scripture. It **surely** doesn't say God can't use a sinner to **write** His inspired Originals or **there would be no Bible**!

Where the Bible is silent we use logic. But **we must remember** that logic is not oracle. Our opinion is not divinely sanctified, so it is nothing more than a sinner's opinion, and is not doctrine. For that reason I could say that this charge is just an argument of logic, but, unfortunately it isn't even **that** sincere. Although **all men are sinners**, the wicked, vile, dishonest state of a man's evil nature truly manifests itself when they stoop to using a fake argument against the Bible which they themselves don't even believe.

QUESTION #87

You want logic? Try this. Which do you think is the greater act, **inspiring** words that have never been written or **preserving** words that have already been written? My logic tells me that **original inspiration** would seem to be the tougher assignment. Well, if so, look at the crew God used to write His words in the first place.

None of the King James translators are reported to have been cold-blooded murderers. Yet, Moses and David were and God used them to **write** his inspired words. None of the King James translators are reported to have been adulterers. David was but God used him to **write** his inspired words. None of the King James translators are reported to have worshipped any God but the God of the Bible. Solomon worshipped false gods & even built houses of worship for them. (1 Kings 11:1-8) None of the King James translators are reported to have publicly denied Jesus Christ. The Apostle Peter did yet God used him to **write** his inspired words.

You might brings these "little" truths to the attention of the next faker who tries to tell you that God couldn't use a sinner to preserve His words!

Question #88

Question: Isn't the King James Bible flawed because the translators didn't capitalize words referring to Deity?

Answer: The King James translators never stated that they were going to capitalize words referring to Deity. You have no right to obligate them to something they never claimed they would do.

Explanation: As a novelty, many modern versions, such as the New King James Version, claim to capitalize words that refer to Deity. That's fine if they wish to make the attempt, but the 1611 King James translators **never said they were doing that** so it is totally unfair and dishonest to criticize them for not doing something they never said they were going to do.

But, as simple a task as this may seem to be, it may be more of a problem than a help. Here are two reasons for having reservations about those versions that claim to capitalize such words:

1. Missing some references - If you read your Bible you know that it states that in John 12:16 and Luke 24:45 that Jesus' own disciples didn't comprehend the prophecies concerning Christ until **after** His resurrection. Thus, **an event** altered what they saw when they read their Bibles. One day they **didn't** see something in a passage and the next day **they**

did. (If you would like to experience this phenomena yourself read Isa 30:25. Now imagine reading that verse on September 10, 2001, and then reading it on September 12, 2001. I'm not even claiming the verse has any connection to what happened on September 11, 2001. I'm simply saying that **an event** can alter what you see in a verse when you read it.)

Now, with that in mind imagine if someone living between the Old and New Testaments said, they were going to print (I **know** there were no printing presses. I said, "imagine.") a Hebrew Bible (our Old Testament) and capitalize all the words that referred to Deity. They would miss **every** prophetic reference to Jesus Christ! They would not see Him in Isaiah 53. They would miss the first verse of Psalm 22 and the reference to His crucifixion in Zechariah 13:6. They would not be aware of the prophecies in Zechariah 11:12, 13.

What if an event happens prior to the Blessed Hope that **reveals** some truth in the Bible that we are blind to now. What if that event reveals references to God in verses where we do not presently see Him. Then those who attempt to capitalize the references to Deity would **miss every one of those references to God** because they wouldn't see them. You say it can't happen? It already did. The event is called the Resurrection!

2. Confusing capitalizations - It is truly amazing how modern translators look down on the King James translators as though they themselves are so vastly superior in intellect and ability. Then they proceed to make countless mistranslations and errors causing problems that simply are not to be found in God' perfect Bible. Following are three such occurrences:

A. The Rock - In 1 Corinthians 10:4 we are told, And did all drink the same spiritual drink: for they drank of that spiritual Rock that followed them: and that Rock was Christ. (This is one of those rare times that the King James translators did capitalize a word referring to God.) In the NKJV, one of those versions that claim to capitalize words referring to Deity, it says, "and all drank the same spiritual drink. For they drank of that spiritual Rock that followed them, and that Rock was Christ." As you can see they capitalized "Rock" since it is plainly referring to God.

Yet when the Lord declares in Matthew 16:18 that He will build His church on the rock, **Himself**, there is **not one modern version** that capitalizes the "rock" to refer to Jesus Christ. I checked seventeen modern versions to see if they capitalized the word "rock" in the verse. By **not** capitalizing it they force Jesus Christ to infer that **Peter** is the "rock," rather than Himself, making the false claim of the Roman Catholic Church valid!

RV, 1881 - ...rock...my church...
ASV, 1901 - ...rock...my church...
RSV, 1952 - ...rock...my church...
NIV, 1973 - ...rock...my church...
NCV, 1987 - ...rock...my church...
NRSV, 1999 - ...rock...my church...
ESV, 2001 - ...rock...my church...
NET, 2007 - ...rock...my church...
CEB, 2011 - ...my church...this rock...

This is bad. These nine modern versions **infer** that Peter is the rock upon which the Lord founded his church. We can be sure the Roman Catholic Church is rejoicing.

But, one truth that is consistent with modern versions is, "No matter how bad they are, it gets worse!" This great truth is born out in the work of the translators of the other eleven modern versions. Not only do they not capitalize "rock" in the verse but they go out of their way to **reenforce** the teaching of the Roman Catholic Church.

The next five versions are similar to the first nine except that they take their subservience to Rome a step further. In these fatally flawed versions the translators capitalized the word "My" when Christ refers to His church so the reader **can't miss** that "rock" applies to Peter rather that Jesus Christ.

NASV, 1960 - ...rock...My church...
NKJV, 1982 - ...rock...My church...
HCSB, 2009 - ...rock...My church...
MEV, 2014 - ...rock...My church...
AmpV, 2015 - ...rock...My church...

If the first nine references can be casually dismissed as "innocent" these five cannot. Note that four out of these five, omitting the Amplified Version, are promoted as conservative versions, as though that label would somehow shield them from the corruptions that infest the so-called liberal translations. Well, we see that that claim is a farce!

The remaining three versions go above and beyond their duty in reassuring their readers that the Roman Catholic claim for Matthew 16:18 is valid. Read and observe how low they bow to the authority of the pope.

GNB, 1966 - And so I tell you, Peter: you are a rock, and on this rock foundation I will build my church,...
CEV, 1995 - So I will call you Peter, which means "a rock." On this rock I will build my church,...
NLT, 2015 - Now I say to you that you are Peter (which means 'rock'), and upon this rock I will build my church,...

B. Deifying the devil - If you think denying the deity of Jesus Christ is a great wrong what do you think of a modern version that **adds deity** to references to the devil? Here are some examples where modern versions capitalized words referring to the devil, thus bestowing on him the attributes of God!

1. Isaiah 14:12

KJB - How art thou fallen from heaven, O Lucifer, son of the morning! how art thou cut down to the ground, which didst weaken the nations!
RSV - How you are fallen from heaven, O Day Star, son of Dawn!
NRSV - How you are fallen from heaven, O Day Star, son of Dawn!
ESV - How you are fallen from heaven, O Day Star, son of Dawn!

Don't even try to excuse this! Even other apostate modern translations refuse to so exalt the devil in such a manner. But they're not finished exalting the devil yet.

2. Zechariah 11:17

KJB - Woe to the idol shepherd that leaveth the flock! the sword shall be upon his arm, and upon his right eye: his arm shall be clean dried up, and his right eye shall be utterly darkened.

In Zechariah 11:17 reference is made to the anti-christ who will terrorize God's people during the Tribulation.

QUESTION #88

First, let me say that the King James Bible is **the only** one that identifies the Anti-Christ as the **"idol"** shepherd. Every modern version eliminates this identification, most calling him the "worthless" shepherd. But three modern versions, one liberal translation and two conservative translations capitalize the reference to this exceedingly evil person.

NASV, 1960 - Who leaves the flock!
NKJV, 1982 - Who leaves the flock!
AmpV, 2015 - Who deserts the flock!

Before you argue the devil's position on this issue (**NEVER** defend the actions of the translators of modern versions!) by claiming they only capitalized it because they put the text in a poetic format therefore the capitalization was required, you'd better check these modern versions: RSV, NIV, CEV, NRSV, ESV, HCSB, MEV and the NLT. **All** of these modern versions **also** put the text in a poetic format and **none** of them capitalized the reference to the devil.

The capitalization hoax is as sincere as a Democrat's promise to help the poor!

Question #89

Question: Modern version translators may not follow the correct line of manuscripts but at least their motives are sincere.

Answer: No, they are not sincere. Do not attribute virtue where there is none.

Explanation: Some of the things modern version translators do cannot be accepted under the label of being "sincere." Examine the examples below and see if you think the actions of these translators could be defined as "sincere." There are many irreconcilable problems with modern versions: Changing "Hell" to "Hades," changing "ass" to "son" in Luke 14:5, or the mixed up mess they turn 1 Samuel 13:1 into. But I will not submit those cases here because someone could, **by a stretch**, claim that these changes do not reflect insincerity because they had the testimony of Greek or Hebrew manuscripts, even if they were corrupt manuscripts.

No, the examples given below cannot be attributed to a sincere translator innocently translating a manuscript that they don't know is corrupt. They are inexcusable and many even fly in the face of even the **corrupt** Greek NT witnesses. If you are prone to being sympathetic or apologetic for modern Bible translators, then ask yourself as you read them if you would accept this kind of strange actions from a doctor, lawyer, or politician.

QUESTION #89

New English Bible - 1970: **"she broke wind"**
KJB - Joshua 15:18 And it came to pass, as she came unto him, that she moved him to ask of her father a field: and she lighted off her ass; and Caleb said unto her, What wouldest thou?
NEB - Joshua 15:18 As she sat on the ass, **she broke wind**, and Caleb asked her , "What did you mean by that?"

KJB - Judges 1:14 And it came to pass, when she came to him, that she moved him to ask of her father a field: and she lighted from off her ass; and Caleb said unto her, What wilt thou?
NEB - Judges 1:14 As she sat on the ass, **she broke wind**, and Caleb said, "What did you mean by that?"

(Even **I** knew what she meant by that!)

There is no excuse for this sacrilegious translation! The Hebrew text doesn't support it nor does any other version on the planet. You must remember, the translation of the Hebrew or Greek text is not done by computers. **Every word** of **every verse** is studied and weighed by a human being before the new translation is committed to ink. Thus, this deplorable translation did not happen by itself while the translators were out having lunch. It was examined and **intentionally** rendered as you read it. And, as if to make sure they had no excuse after perverting Joshua 15:18 they did it a second time in Judges 1:14 just so they had to consider, reconsider and then **commit** to this vile corruption of God's word.

If you find in yourself the desire to defend this action by the NEB translators then, close this book. Your heart is no more honest than the perverts that rendered this vile translation. Until you get right with God nothing you read here will help you.

New King James Version
A. No capital letters

As stated earlier, the translators of the NKJV claimed they capitalized words referring to Deity and they do this numerous times. But there are some **glaring** omissions which betray their lack of faith and even one where they get on their knees and submit to the teaching of the Great Whore of Revelation, the Roman Catholic Church. (I have put the words needing attention in bold.)

Matt 15:5 But you say, 'Whoever says to his father or mother, "Whatever profit you might have received from **me** is a gift to God"

Mark 7:11 But you say, 'If a man says to his father or mother, "Whatever profit you might have received from **me** is Corban"—' (that is, a gift to God),

When the NKJV translators came to these verses in these two gospels where Jesus Christ refers to Himself, they refuse to let Him claim divinity by failing to capitalize the word "me."

If anyone wishes to claim that their plan was to only capitalize words in statements made about Him which were made by others but not by Himself then they will quickly stumble at Luke 24:39 where they did exactly that: Behold **My** hands and **My** feet, that it is I **Myself**. Handle **Me** and see, for a spirit does not have flesh and bones as you see I have.

Four times in one verse they capitalized Jesus' reference to Himself. Now, if you just said, "Well, they didn't capitalize the references in Matthew 15:5 or Mark 7:11 but they got it right in Luke 24." you are so crooked you should go to your local Democratic headquarters and offer yourself as their next candidate for president!

But these two instances pale in comparison to the horrific job they did when translating Matthew 16:18, which reads: And I also say to you that you are Peter, and on this **rock** I will build My church, and the gates of Hades shall not prevail against it.

Never mind the fact that they couldn't bring themselves to acknowledge the existence of Hell. Here, they **openly** embrace the teaching of the Roman Catholic Church, that Christ built his Church on Peter, not Himself, by refusing to capitalize the **plain reference to Christ,** "rock." This lack of capitalization is due to **intentional omission**. How could anyone claim sincerity for the translators of the NKJV? Are they incapable of recognizing a reference made by Jesus Christ to Himself? Would you let a surgeon who was this incompetent operate on you?

B. Diminishing God

It is a very **simple truth** that those who know and serve God wish only to exalt and promote Him and those who are antagonistic towards Him seek only to diminish and lesson His image. Thus, it makes one wonder in just which of these two groups the translators of the NKJV reside when you consider how aggressive they were at deleting references to God or words associated with major doctrines.

The New King James Version omits the following words:

Lord 66 times
God 51 times
heaven 50 times
fornication 23 times
repent 44 times
blood 23 times
JEHOVAH entirely
new testament entirely
hell 22 times
devil 26 times
damnation entirely
soul 137 times

C. Gender exclusion

Removing gender from the Bible as well as from our society is a major part of the agenda of God-hating liberals. Since these people are affected with the mental illness of liberalism they always **say** the opposite of what they **do**. Therefore when they **exclude** gender from the Bible they say they are being inclusive when in **fact** they are being exclusive.

Whereas translations that are to be marketed to liberals make much ado of removing gender, the NKJV, which clearly targets a **conservative** Christian audience never breathed a word of the fact that the NKJV is **more gender exclusive** than the NIV! Why? Because they knew if conservatives knew their translation was gender exclusive they couldn't be fooled into buying it. (How's **that** for sincerity?!)

In just the book of 1 Corinthians gender has been excluded **forty-three times** but no one is ever told that about it.

1 Corinthians	**AV 1611**	**NKJV**
1:26	wise men	wise
2:4	man's wisdom	human wisdom
2:11	no man	no one
2:15	no man	no one
3:5	every man	each one
3:8	every man	each one
3:10	every man	each one
3:11	no man	anyone
3:12	any man	anyone
3:13	Every man's	each one
3:14	any man's	anyone's
3:15	any man's	anyone's
3:17	any mans	anyone
3:18	no man	no one
3:18	any man	anyone

3:21	no man	no one
4:2	a man	one
4:3	man's judgement	human court
4:5	every man	each one's
4:6	*of men*	(deleted)
4:14	sons	children
5:11	any man	any one
7:17	every man	each one
7:18	any man	each one
7:36	flower of her age	of youth
8:2	any man	anyone
8:3	any man	anyone
9:15	any man	anyone
9:25	every man	each one
10:24	no man	no one
10:28	any man	anyone
11:16	any man	anyone
11:34	any man	anyone
12:3	no man	no one
12:3	no man	no one
12:7	every man	each one
12:11	every man	each one
14:2	no man	no one
14:20	be men	be mature
15:23	every man	each one
15:35	some man	some one
16:11	no man	no one
16:22	any man	anyone

If the translators of the NKJV excluded gender **sincerely** they wouldn't have felt compelled to keep it a secret from the public.

(Author's note: The New International Version Inclusive (NIVi) does not remove the **female** gender from 1 Cor. 7:36 while the NKJV does, making the NKJV **more** gender exclusive than the terrible NIVi. Since the publishers of modern versions make changes to the text without informing the public, this may have changed in later editions of the NIVi.)

New International Version
"We need to make more changes or we won't merit a copyright."

Some years ago a man approached me and told me that he was not a translator but a secretary to the translation of the NIV. He said that after several times through the process the translator in charge rebuked his fellow translators because they hadn't made **enough** changes to the text to merit a copyright. He said that eight hundred changes had to be made to qualify for its own copyright so with that "sincere" goal in mind they went back to work until they had achieved the required number of changes. Now **that's** sincerity for you!

NIV & CEV
"Aramaic" for "Hebros"

The NIV was the first modern version to **inexcusably** place the word "Aramaic" in the English text instead of the correct "Hebrew" for the Greek word "Hebros." This was done **everywhere** the word was used to in reference to the Hebrew language, thus underscoring the Roman Catholic Church's assertion that Jesus spoke Aramaic, rather than Hebrew, so they can twist His words to make Peter the "rock" of Matthew 16:18

The NIV inserted this pro-Roman Catholic reading in the divine text of Scripture in 1973. Then in 1995 the Contemporary English Version followed suit. They were joined by the New English Translation in 2007, the Common English Bible in 2011 and then the Amplified Version of 2015. (The original Amplified Version of 1965 correctly translated "Hebros.")

No sincere translator could justify translating "Hebros" anything but "Hebrew," and they certainly would understand that **the only reason** for inserting this fraudulent translation would be to reinforce the false teaching of the Roman Catholic Church.

Of course, all of these corrupt versions correctly translate "Hebros" as "Hebrew" in Philippians chapter three, where Paul refers to himself as a "Hebrew of the Hebrews" showing that they were not ignorant of how the word should be rendered. No honest person can call this kind of translating "sincere."

Original Living Bible

The original edition of the Living Bible, first published in 1971, had King Saul calling his son, Jonathan, in 1 Samuel 20:30, "You son of a b—h!" Mind you, Kenneth Taylor, the producer of this perverted version said he wrote it **for his children**. If you think that's good teaching for your children you are an unfit parent.

Multiple problems with Modern Versions
1 John 5:7

Although the producers of modern versions innocently claim they agree with the King James Bible 99% of the time, a diligent study reveals that that seemingly insignificant 1% change consistently eliminates or waters-down a major Bible doctrine. Apparently the doctrine of the Trinity does not sit well with these self-important translators for it is consistently removed in most modern versions.

Usually when a modern version deletes a verse they don't even bother to cover it up. Most modern version users aren't Bible readers so the theft is unlikely to be discovered. They simply jump from one verse number to the one after the deleted verse. (i.e.: Matt. 17:21, 18:11 & Acts 8:37 just to name a few.) But, knowing that 1 John 5:7 is a verse of such major importance to Christianity the translators of every modern version seek to cover up their theft by splitting either verse 6 or verse 8 to produce a false verse 7. This is **intentionally deceitful** and **cannot** be described by any honest person as "sincere." (Notice below how the translators of the NRSV even broke with the compatriots of the earlier RV & RSV.)

KJB - 1 Jn 5:7 For there are three that bear record in heaven, the Father, the Word, and the Holy Ghost: and these three are one.

ASV - 1 Jn 5:7 And it is the Spirit that beareth witness, because the Spirit is the truth. (Splits v. 6)

ESV - 1 Jn 5:7 For there are three that testify: (Splits v. 8)

HCSB - 1 Jn 5:7 For there are three that testify: (Splits v. 8)

NASV77 - 1 Jn 5:7 And it is the Spirit who bears witness, because the Spirit is the truth. (Splits v. 6)

NASV95 - 1 Jn 5:7 For there are three that testify: (Splits v. 8)

NIV2011 - 1 Jn 5:7 For there are three that testify: (Splits v. 8)

NKJV - 1 Jn 5:7 For there are three that bear witness in heaven: the Father, the Word, and the Holy Spirit; and these three are one. (Renders the verse correctly)

NLT - 1 Jn 5:7 So we have these three witnesses— (Splits v. 8)

RV - 1 Jn 5:7 And it is the Spirit that beareth witness, because the Spirit is the truth. (Splits v. 6)

RSV - 1 Jn 5:7 And the Spirit is the witness, because the Spirit is the truth. (Splits v. 6)

NRSV - 1 Jn 5:7 There are three that testify: (Splits v. 8)

QUESTION #89

MEV - 1 Jn 5:7 There are three who testify in heaven: the Father, the Word, and the Holy Spirit, and the three are one. (Renders the verse correctly)

If this blatant deceitfulness were committed in a **legal contract** these translators would go to prison, but instead, **they go the bank!**

Galatians 5:12

KJB - Gal. 5:12 I would they were even cut off which trouble you.

ASV - Gal. 5:12 I would that they that unsettle you would even go beyond circumcision.

ESV - Gal. 5:12 I wish those who unsettle you would emasculate themselves!

HCSB - Gal. 5:12 I wish those who are disturbing you might also get themselves castrated!

NASV77 - Gal. 5:12 Would that those who are troubling you would even mutilate themselves.

NASV95 - Gal. 5:12 I wish that those who are troubling you would even mutilate themselves.

NIV2011 - Gal. 5:12 As for those agitators, I wish they would go the whole way and emasculate themselves!

NKJV - Gal. 5:12 I could wish that those who trouble you would even cut themselves off!

NLT - Gal. 5:12 I just wish that those troublemakers who want to mutilate you by circumcision would mutilate themselves.

RV - Gal. 5:12 I would that they which unsettle you would even cut themselves off.

RSV - Gal. 5:12 I wish those who unsettle you would mutilate themselves!

NRSV - Gal. 5:12 I wish those who unsettle you would castrate themselves!

MEV - Gal. 5:12 I wish that those who are troubling you would castrate themselves!

There are two points to be noted in the abominable work performed by the translators of **every** modern version, whether they claim to be liberal or conservative. In light that **throughout** the Bible the words "cut off" were meant to represent someone who had violated one of Israel's religious practices and was to be "cut off" from, or **put out** of the congregation. (Check the Old Testament examples on your own. Don't be lazy.) So where do the **minds** of the translators of modern versions constantly dwell that when they see the phrase "cut off" they think of some perverted sexual practice? (If you use a modern version they are **your** trusted translators, not mine!)

The second thing to be noted is that even the so-called "conservative" translations, NKJV, MEV join in this perverted view of the verse. (Are you willing to defend these perverted translations? Good, then you will have to **convince yourself** that the Holy Spirit of God wanted the Apostle Paul to tell men to "castrate themselves!")

2 Timothy 3:3

We all know what "without natural affection" describes several perverted conditions, from homosexuals to religious environmentalist who cry over dead whales but preach that murdering babies is a mother's right. God loaded the gun of Bible preachers to rebuke these perverts by putting 2 Timothy in the text of Scripture...and modern translators not only **unloaded** that gun but reloaded it and aimed it at the very men God called to preach this truth! The Greek word translated "without natural affection" can only be **correctly** translated one way, "no natural affection." But the translators of modern versions, conservative or liberal, stand united against God's condemnation of such perverted practices by inserting a multitude of renderings with **no Greek authority** whatsoever. (Do they have some unnatural affections of their own and feel the sting of the of God's **true words** and were seeking to duck the Holy Spirit's condemnation?) The following modern version readings **can not** be defended as "sincere."

I have reproduced the verses in their entirety so you can see how else the apostate practices of these final days have been clouded over in modern versions.

KJB - 2 Tim. 3:3 Without natural affection, trucebreakers, false accusers, incontinent, fierce, despisers of those that are good,

ASV - 2 Tim. 3:3 without natural affection, implacable, slanderers, without self-control, fierce, no lovers of good,

ESV - 2 Tim. 3:3 heartless, unappeasable, slanderous, without self-control, brutal, not loving good,

HCSB - 2 Tim. 3:3 unloving, irreconcilable, slanderers, without self-control, brutal, without love for what is good,

NASV77 - 2 Tim. 3:3 unloving, irreconcilable, malicious gossips, without self-control, brutal, haters of good,

NASV95 - 2 Tim. 3:3 unloving, irreconcilable, malicious gossips, without self-control, brutal, haters of good,

NIV2011 - 2 Tim. 3:3 without love, unforgiving, slanderous, without self-control, brutal, not lovers of the good,

NKJV - 2 Tim. 3:3 unloving, unforgiving, slanderers, without self-control, brutal, despisers of good,

NLT - 2 Tim. 3:3 They will be unloving and unforgiving; they will slander others and have no self-control. They will be cruel and hate what is good.

RV - 2 Tim. 3:3 without natural affection, implacable, slanderers, without self-control, fierce, no lovers of good,
RSV - 2 Tim. 3:3 inhuman, implacable, slanderers, profligates, fierce, haters of good,
NRSV - 2 Tim. 3:3 inhuman, implacable, slanderers, profligates, brutes, haters of good,
MEV - 2 Tim. 3:3 without natural affection, trucebreakers, slanderers, unrestrained, fierce, despisers of those who are good,

(Author's note: The reader will notice that many modern versions in their original editions followed the King James Bible readings, but as following revisions were produced the translators grew bolder in their wholesale attack on Bible truth. i.e.: ASV cf NASV & RV cf RSV & NRSV)

John 18:36

In this verse Jesus **plainly** states that His future kingdom on this earth is a prophetic reality when He tells Pilate, "...but **now** is my kingdom not from hence."

The Greek word for now, "nun" is found in **every** extant New Testament manuscript that contains John 18:36 yet the translators of most modern versions inexcusably delete the word thus **eliminating** any prophecy of Christ having a literal, visible, earthly kingdom. (Oh, very "sincere!")

KJB - John 18:36 Jesus answered, My kingdom is not of this world: if my kingdom were of this world, then would my servants fight, that I should not be delivered to the Jews: but **now** is my kingdom not from hence.
ASV - John 18:36 "Jesus answered,...but **now** is my kingdom not from hence." (Correct)
ESV - John 18:36 "Jesus answered, ...But my kingdom is not from the world."
HCSB - Jn 18:36 "...My kingdom does not have its origin here."

NASV77 - Jn 18:36 "Jesus answered,...My kingdom is not of this realm."
NASV95 - Jn 18:36 "Jesus answered,...My kingdom is not of this realm."
NIV2011 - Jn 18:36 "Jesus said, But **now** my kingdom is from another place." (Correct)
NKJV - Jn 18:36 "Jesus answered, but **now** My kingdom is not from here." (Correct)
NLT - Jn 18:36 "Jesus answered,...But my Kingdom is not of this world."
RV - Jn 18:36 "Jesus answered,...but **now** is my kingdom not from hence." (Correct)
RSV - Jn 18:36 "Jesus answered,...but my kingship is not from the world."
NRSV - Jn 18:36 "Jesus answered,...But as it is, my kingdom is not from here."
MEV - Jn 18:36 "Jesus answered,...But **now** My kingdom is not from here." (Correct)

The phrase, "only begotten"

The phrase "only begotten" is found only six times in Scripture, all are in the New Testament. Five of those are references to Jesus Christ being God's only begotten Son while Hebrews 11:17 is not a reference to Jesus Christ at all but refers to Genesis 22 when God called for Abraham to offer his "only begotten" Isaac to Him on Mt. Moriah.

The word translated "only begotten" is the Greek word monogenes: mono- "one" or "only" combined in conjunction with genes - "generated" or "begotten." (**Remember!** We **do not** "go to the Greek" as our authority. All it offers is a

second witness to the truth already reveled in the text of our English Bible.)

According to the truth of John 1:12, But as many as received him, to them gave he power to become **the sons of God**, even to them that believe on his name: we find that **everyone** who trusts Christ as their personal Saviour becomes a "son of God." Thus, God has had **millions** of sons born to Him **spiritually** over the centuries since Christ died on the cross and rose again. But Jesus was the only Son God had Who was "begotten" **in the flesh**. Thus, by using the word "monogenes" the Holy Spirit made a differentiation between we who were **spiritually** begotten and He who was **physically** begotten.

In their rendering of the word "monogenes" the translators of modern versions prove they can do something that God never did...**put a contradiction in the Bible!** These modern translators display less knowledge of the Greek language than a first-year Bible college student in their handling of this **not insignificant** word by deleting the description of Jesus being God's only **begotten** Son, thus creating a contradiction between John 1:12 and every reference where He is identified as God's only "begotten" Son.

(Author's note: I have placed Hebrews 11:17 ahead of all the references the Apostle John made to Jesus being God's "only begotten Son" because the appearance of this phrase in the Book of Hebrews is the **first time** that phrase ever appeared in Scripture since Hebrews precedes John's writings by 15 years.)

1. Hebrews 11:17

KJB - By faith Abraham, when he was tried, offered up Isaac: and he that had received the promises offered up **his only begotten son,**

ASV - "...**his only begotten son;**"
ESV - "...his only son,"
HCSB - "...his unique son,"
NASV77 - "...**his only begotten son;**"
NASV95 - "...**his only begotten son;**"
NIV2011 - "...his one and only son,"
NKJV - "...**his only begotten son,**"
NLT - "...his only son, Isaac,"
RV - "...**his only begotten son;**"
RSV - "...his only son,"
NRSV - "...his only son,"
MEV - "...**his only begotten son.**"
(Notice how the translation work of the "Revised" versions corrupted the reading after the initial edition had it correct.)

2. John 1:14
KJB - And the Word was made flesh, and dwelt among us, (and we beheld his glory, the glory as of **the only begotten of the Father**,) full of grace and truth.
ASV - "...**the only begotten from the Father**),"
ESV - "...the only Son from the Father,"
HCSB - "...the One and Only Son from the Father,"
NASV77 - "...**the only begotten from the Father**,"
NASV95 - "...the only begotten from the Father,"
NIV2011 - "...the one and only Son, who came from the Father,"
NKJV - "...**the only begotten of the Father**,"
NLT - "...the Father's one and only Son."
RV - "...**the only begotten from the Father**),"
RSV - "...the only Son from the Father."
NRSV - "...a father's only son,"
MEV - "...the only Son of the Father,"

(Notice that the MEV, which some claim is a modern English rendition of the KJB joins the ranks of the liberal readings.)

3. John 1:18

KJB - No man hath seen God at any time; **the only begotten Son**, which is in the bosom of the Father, he hath declared him.

ASV - "...**the only begotten Son**,"

ESV - No one has ever seen God; the only God, who is at the Father's side, he has made him known. (I've reproduced the entire verse since, although it does not properly translate the verse, it does seem to infer to the deity of Jesus Christ.)

HCSB - "...The One and Only Son"

NASV77 - "...the only begotten God,"

NASV95 - "...the only begotten God," (This and the previous reference make Jesus a begotten "God" which would imply that He was **not** Deity in eternity but only became so once He was begotten in the flesh. An error.)

NIV2011 - "...but the one and only Son,"

NKJV - "...**The only begotten Son**,"

NLT - "...the one and only Son"

RV - "...**the only begotten Son**,"

RSV - "...the only Son,"

NRSV - "...the only Son,"

MEV - "...The only Son,"

4. John 3:16

KJB - For God so loved the world, that he gave **his only begotten Son,** that whosoever believeth in him should not perish, but have everlasting life.

ASV - "...**his only begotten Son,**"

ESV - "...his only Son,"

HCSB - "...His One and Only Son,"
NASV77 - "...**His only begotten Son,**"
NASV95 - "...**His only begotten Son,**"
NIV2011 - "...his one and only Son,"
NKJV - "...**His only begotten Son,**"
NLT - "...his one and only Son,"
RV - "...**his only begotten Son,**"
RSV - "...his only Son,"
NRSV - "...his only Son,"
MEV - "...**His only begotten Son,**"

5. John 3:18
KJB - He that believeth on him is not condemned: but he that believeth not is condemned already, because he hath not believed in the name of **the only begotten Son of God**.
ASV - "...**the only begotten Son of God**."
ESV - "...the only Son of God."
HCSB - "...the One and Only Son of God."
NASV77 - "...**the only begotten Son of God**."
NASV95 - "...**the only begotten Son of God**."
NIV2011 - "...God's one and only Son."
NKJV - "...**the only begotten Son of God**."
NLT - "...God's one and only Son."
RV - "...**the only begotten Son of God**."
RSV - "...the only Son of God."
NRSV - "...the only Son of God."
MEV - "...**the only begotten Son of God**."

6. 1 John 4:9
KJB - In this was manifested the love of God toward us, because that God sent **his only begotten Son** into the world, that we might live through him.
ASV - "...**his only begotten Son**"
ESV - "...his only Son"
HCSB - "...His One and Only Son"
NASV77 - "...**His only begotten Son**"
NASV95 - "...**His only begotten Son**"
NIV2011 - "...his one and only Son"
NKJV - "...**His only begotten Son**"
NLT - "...his one and only Son"
RV - "...**his only begotten Son**"
RSV - "...his only Son"
NRSV - "...his only Son"
MEV - "...**his only begotten Son**"

These examples illustrate why no one with any honesty could believe that what modern translators did to the word of God could be labeled as "sincere."

Question #90

Question: Are the criticisms of the KJB fair?

Answer: No.

Explanation: They are not fair because they are never applied to other versions.

Some of the criticisms of the KJB sound sincere until you also apply them to modern versions.

One example is the sincere-sounding, "I don't like the King James bible because it has words in italics which were added by the translators." This sounds sincere but there is only one way to find out if the person making this statement **truly is** bothered by words in italics. Take them to one of several modern versions that **follow the same practice as the King James Bible.**

Example #1: 2 Thessalonians 2:3

2 Thess 2:3 (KJB) - Let no man deceive you by any means: for *that day shall not come*, except there come a falling away first, and that man of sin be revealed, the son of perdition;

Here we see that the "nasty" King James Bible translators added *"that day shall not come"* in italics for which they are soundly condemned by seemingly sincere, distraught critics. Yet these same "sincere" critics have nothing negative to say about the following modern versions whose translators **did the very same thing!** Condemning the KJB for having italicized words but not the others is like trying to impeach a president for a phone call to Ukraine but saying nothing about another president who sells guns to Mexican drugs lords!

2 Thess 2:3 (ASV) - let no man beguile you in any wise: for *it will not be,* except the falling away come first, and the man of sin be revealed, the son of perdition,

2 Thess 2:3 (NASB77) - Let no one in any way deceive you, for *it will not come* unless the apostasy comes first, and the man of lawlessness is revealed, the son of destruction,

2 Thess 2:3 (NASB) - Let no one in any way deceive you, for *it will not come* unless the apostasy comes first, and the man of lawlessness is revealed, the son of destruction,

2 Thess 2:3 (NKJV) - Let no one deceive you by any means; for *that Day will not come* unless the falling away comes first, and the man of sin is revealed, the son of perdition,

But, apparently modern translators think Americans are so small-minded that all they have to do is **add the words without putting them in italics** and no one will notice. (But you're not that stupid, are you? Are you?) I will place them in bold type below to show they were, indeed, added but simply not italicized.

2 Thess 2:3 (ESV) - Let no one deceive you in any way. For **that day will not come,** unless the rebellion comes first, and the man of lawlessness is revealed, the son of destruction,

2 Thess 2:3 (NIV2011) - Don't let anyone deceive you in any way, for **that day will not come** until the rebellion occurs and the man of lawlessness is revealed, the man doomed to destruction.

2 Thess 2:3 (NLT) - Don't be fooled by what they say. For **that day will not come** until there is a great rebellion against God and the man of lawlessness is revealed—the one who brings destruction.

QUESTION #90

2 Thess 2:3 (HCSB) - Don't let anyone deceive you in any way. For ⌊**that day**⌋ will not come unless the apostasy comes first and the man of lawlessness is revealed, the son of destruction.

Please don't believe me! Put your remote down and open up a few modern versions and compare them to a King James and you'll see the critics of the King James Bible are more hypercritical than the Democrats.

Thus, we see that those who criticize the King James Bible are **not sincere**. They are simply trying to veil their hatred for God's word in what they hope is suitable camouflage for that hatred.

Since they don't really believe what they said. They're being politicians, not preachers.

Appendix

This is a list of common English versions, some which preceded the King James Bible and most which followed after it, as referred to in this book.

1. Wycliff Bible - 1380
2. Tyndale Bible, (NT) - 1525
3. Coverdale Bible - 1535
4. Matthews Bible - 1537
5. The Great Bible - 1538
6. Taverner's Bible - 1539
7. Geneva Bible - 1560
8. The Bishops' Bible - 1568
9. The Douay Rheims - 1582
10. AV or **KJB**, King James Bible - 1611
11. RV, Revised Version - 1881
12. ASV, American Standard Version - 1901
13. RSV, Revised Standard Version - 1952
14. NASV, New American Standard Version - 1960
15. AmpV, Amplified Version - 1965
16. TEV, (Today's English Version), Good News Bible - 1966
17. TEB, New English Bible - 1970
18. LB, The Living Bible - 1971
19. NIV, New International Version - 1973
20. NKJV, New King James Version - 1982

21. **NCV,** New Century Version - 1987
22. **CEV,** Contemporary English Version - 1995
23. **NRSV,** New Revised Standard Version - 1999
24. **ESV,** English Standard Version - 2001
25. **NET,** New English Translation - 2007
26. **HCSB,** Holman Christian Standard Bible - 2009
27. **CEB,** Common English Bible - 2011
28. **MEV,** Modern English Version - 2014
29. **NLT,** New Living Translation - 2015
30. **AmpV15,** Amplified Version - 2015

Other helpful books from:
DayStar Publishing

* A Charted History of the Bible*

By James Kahler. The first book every Christian should have to help them understand how we got our Bible. Easy to read charts with brief, but informative, synopsis on important events in the history of the Bible.

* Gipp's Understandable History of the Bible *

By Samuel C. Gipp. A thorough study of the history of the Bible with information on King James, the translators, where Bible manuscripts came from, the Greek witnesses and numerous comparisons of various modern versions.

* Bread of Life *

By Ted Warmack. A wonderfully complete general study of the Bible covering numerous subjects of interest to Christians, both old and new. Workbook sized and easy to read. Also available in Spanish.

* Living With Pain *

By Samuel C. Gipp. Millions live in constant pain everyday. Dr. Gipp, who has suffered a broken neck has lived with daily pain for over four decades. In this book he helps those who are hurting to deal with their pain.

* Life's Great Moments *

By Jim White. We've all heard of "Murphy's Law." Jim White says, "Murphy was an optimist!" Read about the most amazing and hilarious happenings in this man's life.

***Your Purpose for Existing ***

By Samuel C. Gipp. Ever wonder why God put you on earth? Ever wonder what your purpose for existing is? This book will help you know what you should be doing every single day of your life. A must read for all Christians.

*** Old Paths Preaching Methods ***

By James A. Lince. Before he went home to be with the Lord Bro. Lince recorded and published this work which has been a real help to both preachers and Christians.

Is Our English Bible Inspired?

By Samuel C. Gipp. Has God's divine act of inspiration continued in the King James Bible that we hold in our hand or has His divine inspiration evaporated as the Bible traveled across time?

*** Rightly Dividing God's Word ***

By Victor Shingler. Another look at how to correctly interpret Scripture.

*** Corruptions in the New King James Bible ***

By Jack Munday. Many Christians are fooled into thinking the NKJV is a King James Bible without the "thee's" and "thou's." Jack Munday exposes the drastic changes found in the New King James Version.

*** The Answer Book ***

By Samuel C. Gipp. This book has become a classic. It answers over 60 charges brought against the King James Bible. In publication for almost two decades,. it is still in great demand. Nothing in this book has been refuted.

*** Fight On!, More Fight On! Stories***

By Samuel C. Gipp. Short, one-page, stories which will encourage the reader to "Fight On!" as others have before them. *More Fight On! Stories* continues the series.

*** Why We Believe the King James Bible ***

By Samuel C. Gipp. Under 40 pages this little booklet gives the truth seeker a brief explanation as why Bible believers believe there is a perfect Bible on this earth.

*** The Certainty of the Words ***

By Kyle Stevens. The is over 700 pages attesting to the supremacy of the King James Bible.

*** *Valiant for the Truth* ***

A two-year course suitable for Christian schools, home schoolers, Bible institutes, Youth Groups or individuals who simply want to be able to answer those who relentlessly attack the authority of their Bible. Produced in two series, 11 and 12, each series contains twelve lessons that simplify the most difficult answers to questions about the authority of the King James Bible.

DayStar also has sermons and lessons on CD and DVD as well as over a dozen posters for kids. Fifteen of the posters have been reproduced as postcards.

DayStarPublishing.com or call: **1-800-311-1823**